Axis of Influence

Axis of Influence

How Credibility & Likeability Intersect to Drive Success

Michael Lovas & Pam Holloway

New York

Axis of Influence
How Credibility & Likeability Intersect to Drive Success

ISBN 978-1-60037-534-7

Library of Congress Control Number: 2008941334

MORGAN · JAMES
THE ENTREPRENEURIAL PUBLISHER

Morgan James Publishing, LLC
1225 Franklin Ave., STE 325
Garden City, NY 11530-1693
Toll Free 800-485-4943
www.MorganJamesPublishing.com

In an effort to support local communities, raise awareness and funds, Morgan James Publishing donates one percent of all book sales for the life of each book to Habitat for Humanity. Get involved today, visit **www.HelpHabitatForHumanity.org.**

Contents

Introduction

The axis we refer to in the title is a standard X/Y axis, but it is populated by very uncommon elements. If you picture X as Credibility and Y as Likeability, you can actually track or measure how effective you are with your chosen target audiences. The more you have of each, the more influential you can be. The more influential you are, the more successful you can become.

I suppose we all find ourselves from time to time showing off our knowledge, which might get us points in Credibility but not in Likeability. Other times we charm people with our jokes or bright smile, which may score us Likeability points but do nothing for our Credibility. Only when we combine both sides of the axis do we find ourselves at our most powerful. To dominate our markets, we must show ourselves as being high in Likeability and high in Credibility at the same time.

In the early nineties I (ML) began writing about Credibility. I simply did what I thought was logical. I interviewed people I perceived as highly credible and asked them two questions: How did you get there (in other words, what did you do to establish your Credibility?)? And what impact did it have on your bottom line? The answers were consistent from everyone.

Each person said that writing a book had the biggest impact on his or her Credibility. Those who hadn't yet published their book noted that articles, reports, white papers or delivering speeches had served to build their Credibility. The consistent answer to bottom-line impact was 50 percent. Their businesses improved by 50 percent as a direct result of these Credibility activities. They had achieved one part of the Axis of Influence.

This information prompted me to combine my marketing, writing and coaching skills into a new company called Credibility Marketing. For more than a decade we focused on helping professionals demonstrate their Credibility. The majority of people we worked with were in fact credible, but suffered from a disconnect between perception and reality. In other words, their Credibility was not obvious to the people they were looking to attract.

We helped solve that disconnect by getting the expertise out of their heads and into a form they could use. We showed them how to use their Credibility as a differentiator. We helped them transition from *chase* marketing to *attract* marketing. When Credibility Marketing is used effectively, it means clients find you and self-select to do business with you. This is vastly preferable to the alternative—you continually chasing after people, hoping to find those who will buy what you're selling. Credibility Marketing is a much more effective approach, isn't it?

We started writing a book on Credibility in the early nineties but set it aside because we weren't able to find enough hard evidence to substantiate the impact of Credibility. As compelling as it is, anecdotal evidence by itself is really of little value. This began to change in 1995–96 with the publication of Kouzes' and Posner's book *Credibility: How Leaders Gain and Lose it, Why People Demand It.* Their book is more for managers rather than sales professionals, but it helped the concept of Credibility gain a foothold. Over time researchers began to take a scientific look at related concepts including perceptions of competence and trustworthiness.

We continued to write about Credibility. We also began to develop tools and techniques that we taught in our classes and used in our coaching. Although we had many success stories, we had a sense that something was missing. We began to ask ourselves, "Is Credibility enough?"

We decided to take an even closer look at the characteristics of the highly successful and see if we could identify the *what else*. After analyzing many world-class professionals, we found the missing ingredient. It is *Likeability*.

Like us, I'm sure you know people who are highly credible but, for whatever reason, just aren't particularly likeable. Likewise you know people who are likeable but not particularly credible. It's the combination of Credibility and Likeability that separates the great from the pretty good.

With that bit of wisdom in mind, we decided to address both topics in this book. They are in fact two sides of the *success equation*—sort of the yin and yang of success in business relationships. They are also related in two other ways: the determination of both is made primarily by other people, not you; and the determination is made quickly in the other person's subconscious mind.

Because the subconscious is a messy, illogical environment where subjective perception is more important than reality, the determination of your Credibility and Likeability is not always logical. Perhaps the most important nugget of truth in this book is that the actual levels of your Credibility and Likeability are secondary to what other people perceive about you. Their perception *is* reality.

If you want to understand how to improve the way other people see, hear and experience you, then you're in luck. That's exactly what you're going to learn in these pages.

As coaches, consultants and trainers, we love helping professionals improve their Credibility and Likeability. We believe it's where the real action is! We wish you the best in your own quest to become more credible and likeable.

— Michael Lovas and Pam Holloway

Chapter 1:
Why Are Credibility &
Likeability Important to You?

When we set out to study Credibility and Likeability, our first objective was to see if these elements really had the impact we initially thought. We were delighted to find ample research to support our initial conclusions. Bottom line—people who are credible as well as likeable can achieve more success in both business and personal life. This is true of all people and professions, but it is especially true for consultants, advisors, sales people and politicians—businesses in which personal relationships are critically important. If that's you, your success is directly dependent upon your ability to get people to listen to you, like you, believe you, and trust you.

The following pages enumerate some of the gems we've discovered that validate the importance of Credibility and Likeability. Beyond that, we will show you how to improve both!

1. Success in the *Workplace* is Linked to Likeability and Credibility

Look around the business world at the men and women at the top and you'll find plenty of evidence to support the notion that Credibility, or at least the perception of Credibility, is a key enabler of success. We are drawn to and tend to follow those who have a commander-in-chief demeanor. There is even a *look of Credibility* among the most successful, which we discuss in more detail later in the book. Suffice it to say, workplace success is linked to Credibility.

Likeability is also important, perhaps even more important. *Harvard Business Review* authors Casciaro and Lobo In *Fool vs. Jerk: Whom Would You Hire?* note that both Likeability and competence are important in the workplace, but that Likeability may trump competence.

"We found that if someone is strongly disliked, it's almost irrelevant whether or not she is competent; people won't want to work with her anyway. By contrast, if someone is likeable, his colleagues will seek out every little bit of competence he has to offer. This tendency didn't exist only in extreme cases; it was true across the board. Generally speaking, a little extra likability goes a longer way than a little extra competence in making someone desirable to work with."

So Likeability is critically important to getting along with your colleagues, but is it also important to making your way up the ladder? According to a Columbia University study by Melinda Tamkins, the answer is yes. Tamkins found that success in the workplace is guaranteed not by what or whom you know, but by your popularity (which we suggest is two parts Likeability, one part Credibility).

In her study, Tamkins found that popular workers were seen by their colleagues as trustworthy, motivated, serious, decisive and hardworking. Further, they were recommended for fast-track promotions and generous pay increases. On the flip side, their less-liked colleagues were perceived as arrogant, conniving and manipulative. Pay raises and promotions were ruled out for them, regardless of their academic backgrounds or professional qualifications.

2. Success in *Politics* is Linked to Credibility and Likeability

Think about recent elections. Credibility and Likeability came into play time and again. Remember all the comments about Hillary Clinton's Likeability deficit? She was seen as credible, but apparently Credibility was not enough. Sarah Palin, on the other hand, was seen as highly likeable, but her Credibility was in question. Obama and McCain were relatively close in Credibility scores at the close of the election, but Obama had a 3 to 1 lead in the Likeability department.

We know from the research that Likeability wins elections. The Gallup organization has conducted a Personality Factor poll prior to every presidential election since 1960. They look at three factors: issues, party affiliation, and Likeability. Only one factor has been a consistent prognosticator of the final election result. That factor is Likeability.

Take a look at a few of the elections over the past few decades. Who was more likeable: Reagan or Carter, Clinton or Bush Senior, Bush Junior or John Kerry?

We also found evidence that competence, or at least the perception of competence, wins elections. Research by Alexander Todorov of Princeton University shows that voters tend to choose the candidate who *appears* more competent or credible. This would seem to conflict with the studies saying the more likeable candidate wins. So which is it—competence or Likeability? The truth is both are equally valuable. Credibility wins elections, and so does Likeability.

Unfortunately, we don't yet have the results of any study that accurately measures one against the other. However, anecdotal evidence suggests that all things being equal, Likeability trumps Credibility. The smart money looks to accommodate both sides. After all, they're not mutually exclusive. Rather, when possessed in tandem, they present an exceptionally powerful perception.

3. Success in *Sales* is Linked to Credibility and Likeability

Both Credibility and Likeability are essential traits of personal magnetism and sales success. When the product or service is sophisticated and complex, the Credibility of the messenger becomes more important. However, Credibility by itself is not enough. Customers must also like you.

Mitch Anthony, author of *Selling with Emotional Intelligence*, says, "Clients place as much emphasis on 'likeability' as they do on ability." After interviewing 6,852 decision makers, the late Bill Brooks and the late Tom Travisano said, "Only 17 percent of the decision makers could remember more than one time when they had the option to *not* buy and still went ahead and bought from a salesperson they didn't like."

4. Better *Health Care* Linked to Likeability and Credibility

Likeability and Credibility are not only important to your financial bottom line, but it would appear they are also important to your health. Research suggests that doctors give more time and better care to patients they like and less to those they don't like.

A 1984 University of California study led by Barbara Gerbert found that the combination of likeability and competence affected the care that patients received. Patients perceived as likeable and competent were encouraged a lot more often to telephone and to return more frequently for follow-ups than patients who were seen as either unlikable and competent or likeable and incompetent. In addition, the staff tended to educate the likeable patients significantly more often than the unlikable patients. The likeable, competent patients tended to receive augmented medication more frequently than those seen as less likeable and less competent.

Consider this the next time you visit your doctor or the hospital: the squeaky wheel most likely is getting less grease. The complaining patient is likely to get adequate (but not great) care, and be gently encouraged to find a different provider.

5. Success in *Court* Is Linked to Credibility and Likeability

Likeability and Credibility serve you in the courtroom as well as the workplace and hospital. We know that juries tend to believe defendants, expert witnesses and attorneys they like and perceive as credible. Both elements exert a strong influence on trial outcomes.

Credibility is important with expert witnesses, but Likeability seems to trump Credibility when it comes to jurors' perception of defendants. In fact, research suggests that likeable and believable defendants are less likely to be found guilty. Further, even when found guilty, they are likely to get more lenient sentences than less likeable defendants.

Attorney behavior exerts a strong influence on trial outcomes as well. Attorneys who are able to put themselves in the shoes of jurors and connect with them in a deep and powerful way achieve greater success than those who tend to focus merely on facts. This type of *connection* is a key element of Likeability.

Again, the smart money looks to accommodate both sides. After all, Credibility and Likeability are not mutually exclusive. Rather, when demonstrated in tandem, they give an exceptionally powerful perception.

Chapter 2: The Process:
Trust + Likeability + Credibility = Influence

In March 2008 I (ML) was consulting with a military contractor in Iraq. The contractor was asking about Credibility, specifically how he could prove his Credibility to the Iraqi Army, so they would take his advice. I suggested that he may not be aware of the process he needed to follow. I explained to him that he probably had already demonstrated his competence, but for his work showing competence was putting the cart in front of the Hummer. It wasn't his competence that the Iraqis questioned; it was his trustworthiness. He had not yet proved himself trustworthy to them. Without that trust, they would find him and his advice suspect. Without that trust, they would not be able to predict with certainty that his advice would be appropriate to them 100 percent of the time. There would always be the question—would he sell them out?

In a situation like that, the bottom line is a bit more serious than in a retail-selling situation. Let's say that contractor gained trust and then did not live up to it. In Iraq, he could get shot. What about in the States? There is an argument to be made that the Bush administration failed to live up to its promise, and that's why the Democrats did so well in the 2008 election. What about in American business? What if your firm provides flood insurance but cancels policies when claims are filed? What if your firm provides credit to consumers and cancels the accounts of people with excellent credit? Don't those situations paint a picture of businesses that have failed to live up to the promise of trustworthiness? Have they not breached the trust? Don't they lose any Credibility?

Let's apply that lesson to you and your business. Most of us have met people who are knowledgeable and competent, but we don't care to do business with them. There's just something about them that causes us to keep them at arm's length. This is generally an issue of trust. Trust is fundamental to both Likeability and Credibility:

- Trust is your ticket. Without it, you can't get into the show.

- Once you prove that you're trustworthy, you'll find that both Likeability and Credibility are possible.

- All the Credibility in the world is for naught if you can't make yourself likeable to the people you want to influence.

- When you can combine trust, Likeability and Credibility, you will become the most powerful force.

Likeability and Credibility represent the fulcrum where business teeters one way or the other. Your own business goes up or down based on how adroit you are at building and using your Likeability and Credibility. The question everyone asks is, "How can I get these qualities?" The answer is you don't get them; they're not the result of an event. Instead, you develop them. They are part of a process—a process that begins with trust.

If I trust you, I will be comfortable enough to engage with you a little longer and see if I like you. If I like you, then I'll engage a bit longer and give you a chance to demonstrate your Credibility. If I perceive you as both likeable and credible, you have doubled the odds that I will want to do business with you.

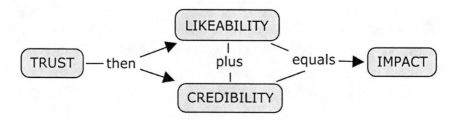

Figure 2-1: Likeability-Credibility Process

We can use that as a formula. Without trust, you won't get far in business. Can you succeed in business if you are perceived as credible but not likeable or likeable but not credible? The answer is "Yes, but ..." If you are credible but lack Likeability, can you be successful? Yes, but not if your business is heavily dependent on relationships. If you are likeable but not perceived as particularly credible, can you be successful? Yes, but not if your business depends on high levels of knowledge and expertise.

Likeability truly is the wild card here. Many people argue that Likeability is not an essential ingredient for success in some professions. Interestingly, the legal profession is the most common example put forth. Let's look deeper into this question. When I hire a lawyer to defend me, or a surgeon to operate on me, or a consultant to revamp my business processes, I simply do not have to like them, as long as they implement their area of expertise.

The question is: if my lawyer were more likeable in addition to being credible, would that improve his or her effectiveness? It would if he or she had to present our case to a judge or jury or anyone else. It certainly influences whether or not I want to spend time around him or her. And that influences whether or not I am likely

Michael Lovas & Pam Holloway

to continue to do business with him or her and recommend him or her to my network of colleagues. The same goes for the surgeon, the consultant and any other professional.

The point is the level of success you achieve and the sustainability of that success are directly tied to both Likeability and Credibility. Without both, you are limited in how far you can go. Put the two together and watch your results spike!

This will make even more sense when we look *under the hood* and see what actually goes on in the brain when people first meet you and make subconscious decisions about you—your trustworthiness, Likeability, and Credibility.

14

Chapter 3:
The Trust Detector

Both Likeability and Credibility begin with the other person's first impression of you. Your parents probably told you to always make a positive first impression. They may have explained that to make that positive first impression you need to comb your hair, straighten your tie and smile when you shake hands. Those little adjustments come into play, and, while important, by themselves they don't do enough to substantially influence that first impression. They are certainly not effective in terms of trust, Credibility, and Likeability.

The first impression is a mental activity that goes on behind the scenes in your *old brain*. To understand how it affects trust, Likeability and Credibility, you have to understand how and why this old brain functions, so let's look at a little biological history.

As we humans developed and evolved, our brains went through a few different phases. Our first brain is called the *old brain*. It is the oldest part of your brain, and it's still there working round-the-clock on your behalf. The old brain's function that is most relevant here is self-preservation. In a world where giant predators with enormous appetites were looking to snack on your body parts, it helped to have that self-preservation function operating in high gear.

Today, every time a stranger looks at you, he or she makes a split-second determination as to your trustworthiness. Will you try to kill him or her or not? Should he or she run or not? Those determinations are made when that stranger looks at your face and demeanor, and they are made very quickly. After all, it's a life-or-death decision. What's more, that stranger then will hold onto that decision, and you'll find it nearly impossible to change his or her mind.

Princeton researcher and professor Alexander Todorov discovered that when we see a new face our brains make split-second judgments on whether or not that person is trustworthy, attractive and competent. Remember, we're talking about your subjective perception of those things, not a consciously logical selection.

Todorov says, "The link between facial features and character may be tenuous at best, but that doesn't stop our minds from sizing other people up at a glance. We decide very quickly whether a person possesses many of the traits we feel are important, such as likeability and competence, even though we have not exchanged a single word with them. It appears that we are hard-wired to draw these inferences in a fast, unreflective way."

Kevin Hogan, author of *The Science of Influence*, explains it this way: "When you first meet someone, millions of neurons in the brain are activated. The unconscious mind goes immediately to work, makes all kinds of judgments and evaluations, and essentially pegs the person a winner or loser in approximately four seconds."

First Impression # 1: Trustworthiness

In one of their studies, Todorov's researchers looked at four qualities: attractiveness, competence, trustworthiness, and aggressiveness. They expected to find that attractiveness was the most important judgment, but they were wrong. They actually discovered that trust is the most important. The implication is, first comes trust—before anything else—only then can we perceive attractiveness or competence.

According to Todorov, this is not particularly surprising, as detection of trustworthiness is part of our evolutionary DNA and essential for human survival. Deciding if a stranger is trustworthy is one of the most important decisions we routinely face. Perceived trustworthiness influences our decision to approach or avoid that person. It also serves as a gatekeeper mechanism for social interactions.

Functional MRIs by Todorov and others suggest that detection of trustworthiness in a face is a spontaneous, automatic process linked to activity in the amygdala (which is part of the old brain). "The fear response involves the amygdala, a part of the brain that existed in animals for millions of years before the development of the prefrontal cortex, where rational thoughts come from," he said. "We imagine trust to be a rather sophisticated response, but our observations indicate that trust might be a case of a high-level judgment being made by a low-level brain structure. Perhaps the signal bypasses the cortex altogether."

You're probably wondering how this is relevant to you in your business. Surely your clients aren't worried that you're going to club them over the head when you walk into their office. Even though there is typically no rational reason for this fear, the amygdala is still hard at work doing its job. The nature of the fear has changed from one of physical safety to one of emotional safety, but the fear response is still there.

Your job, if you want to improve these first impressions, is to recognize this emotional (non-rational) response and make it easier for people to *feel* they can trust you. We'll get into the specifics of how to do that shortly, but first let's examine exactly what someone else's subconscious mind is *reading* when he first meets you.

How Your Face Communicates Trust

Given the evolutionary basis of our face-reading instinct, we know there is self-preservation at work in our initial judgments. Our pre-language old brain quickly scans the face for danger signals. Certain things, perhaps a smile and sparkling eyes, tell us that we can relax, that the other person is safe. On the other hand, a furrowed brow or intense stare sends a warning signal.

This should be especially troubling to you if you are highly analytical or work with someone who is highly analytical. The analytical face tends to show a brooding, serious facial expression that can be interpreted as unfriendly, thus unsafe. That's unfortunate because chances are that face is merely

Figure 3-1: Analytical Face

registering what's going on inside a person's head—he or she is focusing intensely on the information at hand. This is an example of how much perception differs from reality. Look at Figure 3-1 and you'll see that the analytical face does not look particularly inviting.

Baby Face Features Inspire Trust

That leads us to the question of what kind of face causes us to feel safe. According to research by Leslie Zebrowitz of Brandeis University, we make immediate judgments on Likeability, competence and trustworthiness based on the person's face. The more baby-faced the person (characterized by a round face, large eyes, and a small nose and chin), the more likely we are to perceive that person as trustworthy and likeable. After all, how could a little baby be a devious predator? The opposite type of face (more mature and angular) may not be seen as trustworthy, but it is often perceived as more competent. We'll cover this in more detail in the Likeability and Credibility sections.

Take a quick glance at the pictures in Figure 3-2. Which person do you trust more? Look at the faces a second time. Which face looks more likeable? Which looks more credible?

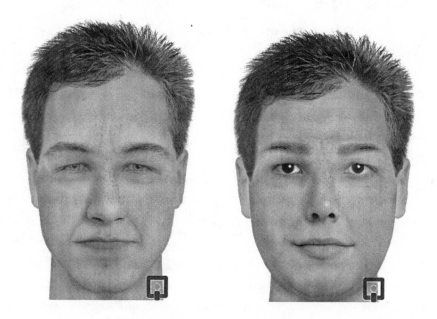

Figure 3-2: Which face do you trust more?

Most people view the face on the right as more likeable and more trustworthy, and the face on the left as more competent. So what can you do if you don't happen to be blessed with a trusting face? Although there's not much you can do to change your facial structure short of cosmetic surgery, there is a great deal you can do to control the "look" of your face. For example, if you have a long, narrow (competent) face, then a genuine smile (in your eyes) will show you as kinder, and a Cheshire-cat grin will give you a rounder chin. In addition, you could raise your eyebrows slightly. That will give you more rounded eyes. Think of your mouth and your eyebrows as being attached. As your mouth moves into a smile, raise your eyebrows an equal amount. That facial expression says, "I'm open and I'm listening." All three of those adjustments can dramatically soften your face and change the overall message given by it.

How Your Demeanor Communicates Trust

Everything we've just explained is directly relevant to your success. Our *trust detector* might be better called a *safety detector*, because that's actually what your old brain is looking for. It's asking, "Am I in danger?" It's deciding whether or not to call out your mental *fight-or-flight* guys. If you can't get past this juncture, you cannot succeed with that person.

Let's say you come into my office to make a sales presentation. As you begin to talk, I go into an unconscious internal discussion with myself over my personal safety. While this process is going on in my head, I am not capable of listening to you or seeing beyond my internal dialog. What that means to you is vital; you have to make me feel safe, before anything else. That's the only way to turn off my automatic responses. You must do that as quickly as possible in order to get me to take the next step, which is to decide whether

I trust you or not. Without safety nothing is possible, but with safety assured, trust is possible. Once trust is established, the door to Likeability is opened.

The Safe Space. In other words, your very first objective is to create a safe space for the other person. This is a space that is both physical and mental, and is typically measured from nose to nose at about four feet.

Physically, we want to give the person space so that we don't make him or her feel trapped. That means not standing over him or her or sitting too close. You'll know right away if you've invaded someone's personal space because he or she will back up or move to place an object between you two. I (ML) was recently talking with a man who had just returned from fighting in Iraq. He was a big, strong guy who was built like a professional boxer. He looked like a recruiting poster. As we talked I kept moving closer to him, and as I did he kept backing up. The point here is a poignant one: you cannot always make an accurate guess about what distance feels safe to another person. That said, you could make an educated guess that four feet is safe and then adjust if necessary.

Picture each of you inside your own bubble. As you talk, both of you move back and forth, kind of like a dance. How close you get is determined by different factors. Here are some facts about the *personal space* bubbles:

- The bubble is larger if you are talking to a stranger. Give extra space and let the other person decide how close is comfortable.

- The better you know the person you're talking to, the smaller the bubble may be. Friends already feel safe with each other.

- The bubble is usually larger for two men than for two women. Men need more distance; they tend to avoid the appearance of intimacy.

- The bubble may be very small for a man and a woman if they are in a relationship.

- The bubble may be larger than normal for a man and a woman who are strangers to each other.

- The higher the status of the person, the larger personal space he or she demands.

- The bubble size is affected by different cultures. Latin cultures, for example, are comfortable with less space. Crowded cultures are comfortable with less space.

- Americans like to keep more open space in between themselves and their conversation partners.

- People who have been in combat or are abuse victims require more space.

Your job is to understand and accommodate the unconscious mental processes going on in the other person's mind. When you understand those processes, and use that knowledge effectively, you can become more influential. This is one way you can improve your safety, thus leading to trust and Likeability.

How You Can Help People Trust You

First step: make yourself safe. Did you ever see any of the Discovery Channel shows about animals fighting? They puff up and try to look as large and intimidating as possible. That's what you'd do too, if you were going to do battle. Trust is the opposite of that, and it includes these elements:

- Smile in your eyes.

- Look directly at the person around the eyes but not into the eyes (no glaring)

- Open trusting posture—open palms

- Sideways tilt of your head

- Nod, and encourage the conversation by saying, "Uh huh … OK … I see"

Why are those postures important? For two reasons: they are the main tools we use to communicate friendliness and trustworthiness, and nonverbal cues carry much more information than verbal ones.

In research published in the February 2006 *European Journal of Social Psychology* we learn that when the verbal and nonverbal cues are somewhat equal, the nonverbal is usually stronger. Bottom line: pay close attention to your nonverbal messages.

Keep your hands to yourself! In our discussion of personal space, we painted a picture of a bubble around you and one around the other person. In our consulting work, we've discovered that many analytical people don't have a good understanding of this personal space. The result is they unwittingly invade the other person's space. For example, one of our coaching clients was in the habit of reaching across the desk and writing on his client's note pad. He lost a lot of business that way.

Be Quiet! Because business is conducted via conversations, another type of personal space has developed. It is the auditory space around you when you talk. The guideline is this: when you talk the other person remains quiet. When he talks you remain quiet. Unfortunately, business is often driven by people with powerful personalities, and they do not like to remain quiet and listen.

They prefer to jump in and move the process forward at a faster clip. That constitutes an invasion of personal (auditory) space. As you would guess, it easily destroys trust and closes the door to Likeability. With that door closed, it is extremely rare that any business can be conducted.

How Similarity & Familiarity Effect Trust

Studies suggest that one of the things we register is similarity. The brain is associative. This means that, in order to interpret the things we come into contact with, we need to find a reference point. We ask ourselves subconsciously, "Do I know this face? Is it familiar to me, my clan, tribe, colleagues or friends?" Familiarity eases trust. A face that is familiar may not belong to someone you actually know. It may mean that you're looking at someone whose face is similar in appearance to someone you know, or even to your own face. The idea is that a face which is similar to that of someone you know, evokes emotions or attitudes associated with the original person.

Although familiarity and similarity are generally positive (i.e., the more I see you, the more attractive and likeable you become), it can work against you as well. If your face registers as familiar to me because you look similar to my crazy Aunt Bert, I will unconsciously assume you have a similar internal makeup as Bert. According to Leslie Zebrowitz in *Reading Faces*, "people who physically resemble each other are perceived to have similar traits."

In a study designed to see how we judge trustworthiness, Lisa DeBruine at the University of Aberdeen in Scotland had volunteers play an online game in which they had to decide whether to trust another player to split a sum of money. All they had to go on was a picture. Volunteers were shown photos of students from another university, and also saw photos that DeBruine had manipulated electronically to incorporate aspects of the volunteer's own face. The manipulations were subtle enough for the volunteers not to notice them, but the effect was remarkable nevertheless. Players were far more likely to trust the faces that incorporated aspects of their own face.

We also make assumptions based on archetypes. A woman who looks like Marilyn Monroe will have a difficult time convincing us of her mental competence. Similarly, a man who looks like Adolf Hitler would have a difficult time making a likeable first impression. We perceive anyone who looks like an archetype to have the same traits and characteristics as that archetype.

What does all of this mean to you? How can you use this information? The answer is as obvious as the nose on your face. To help make yourself more trustworthy, make yourself look like the person in front of you. You do that by mirroring his face. Simply make that person's facial expression back at him.

People are rarely aware of what facial expression they are wearing, but they do recognize certain facial expressions on other people. Those expressions are the ones they wear themselves. If I carry a smile in my eyes all the time, and I see someone else who has that expression, I will immediately understand that we both share something. If the expression is expressive and curious, we will both register the similarity because it is familiar to us. "I know that face. I know what it means. Therefore, I might trust that person."

Dealing with Preconceived Notions

Salespeople tend to make the same mistake: they think they will be the one person with the pitch, logic or closing technique that will change someone's mind from no to yes. Unfortunately, that's just not how brains work. Let's say you're a person whose job is to persuade or influence other people. You might be a recruiter, consultant, preacher, insurance agent, attorney or CPA. If someone you're talking to has a prejudice or presumption about people with your job, you'll have a snowball's chance in Texas of changing his or her mind. It has nothing to do with you or your message. It has everything to do with them—all of them, all humans. Let's see why.

Remember the amygdala? It's part of the old brain that deals with fear. Well, it loves sameness. Let me explain. Imagine you were bitten by a dog when you were a child. You learned very quickly that dogs are dangerous—not just that particular dog, but all dogs, from tiny toy poodles to big mastiffs. It will not be easy to change your mind as you get older. In fact, you'll look to substantiate and justify your fear.

Most of us successfully avoid personal experience with carnivorous animals, but we cannot go through life without reading and hearing news about people being taken advantage of. What thoughts flash in your mind when you think of Enron, Agent Orange, CEO compensation, corporate bailout, increasing insurance premiums, FEMA or taxes?

You have preconceived notions about those dangers, but where did those attitudes come from? Did you get mugged by an Enron manager or attacked by an insurance agent? Probably not, but there is an attitude already resident in your mind, and its job is to protect you from them.

What if I tell you that Enron was framed, insurance companies all have your best interest at heart, CEOs are underpaid and FEMA was the hero of hurricane Katrina? Would you believe me? Probably not, and here's the reason. That information (actually the response to that information) resides in your amygdala, and its job is to protect you. It's not easily going to change its mind about sophisticated dangers, any more than it's going to forget that dogs are dangerous. Some intense fears are totally illogical, but to the person affected by them, they are still very real. Fear of heights, tight spaces, germs, loud noises and falling are very real. When my mother was a child, she had a fear of buttons. A strange fear, but to her it was very real.

What does that have to do with Likeability and Credibility? You can lose Credibility if you don't understand this lesson, or if you forget it in the heat of a presentation. What are some things you can do to prevent this?

- Never try to change the mind of anyone who has a preconceived notion. Rather, agree with the person to some extent by saying things like, "Yes, I think you might be right," or, "I've never gotten the full story on that."

- Ask a follow-up question such as, "Was it Ken Lay or Jeffrey Skilling who did the most damage?" or, "I wonder how much the homeowner insurance companies paid out in Katrina-related claims," or, "If all insurance companies are crooks, why do business with any of them?"

- Get the other person to agree with you on something. "Wouldn't it be great if FEMA could actually deliver on the potential?" or, "I sure would love it if insurance costs were reasonable, wouldn't you?"

The point is, while the other person may have a preconceived notion about major issues, your job title or your industry, he probably doesn't have a prejudice against you. So position yourself differently. Don't be a crusader for the industry. Don't preach. Don't unload your opinions and arguments on him. Doing any of those things would be to smash heads, and that would be fruitless and painful. Be smarter than his amygdala. Build a bridge from person to person. Find something you can agree on and build from there.

If you can find three things that you both agree on, you will have begun to build a *truth frame*, which will build agreement momentum. The more momentum you create, the more trust is built.

Chapter 4:
The Attractiveness Effect

In addition to judgments of safety and trust, the brain also makes immediate judgments of attractiveness. This also has an evolutionary bias. It's leftover from when mate selection and reproduction were high on the list of priorities. Logically, this won't be a consideration in a business meeting, right? Wrong. Remember, this is the emotional brain at work, not the logical brain. So yes, attractiveness is important in business, too. In fact, it is far more important than most people think.

In an article titled "Perceiving Beauty," Dr. Ben Jones, a lecturer in the School of Psychology at the University of Aberdeen, says that a wealth of empirical evidence demonstrates that we not only prefer physically attractive romantic partners and friends, but we also prefer to employ and vote for *beautiful* people.

Attractive People Inherit Other Positive Qualities

Being seen as attractive gives you a lot more than just a stroke to your vanity. There is a great deal of research suggesting that if you are perceived as attractive, you *inherit* other positive qualities regardless of whether you actually posses them or not. In fact, research by Alan Feingold shows that attractive people are seen as smarter, more successful, more sociable, mentally healthier and higher in self-esteem than less attractive people.

Right or wrong, we make immediate judgments about a variety of qualities based on the mere perception of attractiveness. Here's how it works. Someone walks into your office. Bang! You immediately form an opinion of that person that includes a set of additional attributes. How does that happen? Most people possess assumptions about what personality traits go together with attractiveness. In fact, our natural tendency is to heap ever more positive traits onto someone we see as attractive.

The technical term coined for this is *implicit personality theory*. It comes from Harold Kelley's work in social psychology and means that the very first traits we see in a person serve to influence our perception of the other traits. In other words, we are likely to project (or package) positive characteristics onto a person when our first impression of that person is positive. It's as though positive qualities come in a set that cannot be broken up. This is especially true with attractiveness. If we perceive a person as attractive, we extend to him or her many other positive characteristics.

This is also known as the *halo effect*, a term coined by Edward Thorndike in the 1920s. Thorndike did experiments asking military officers to rate their subordinates. He found that people seem to think of other individuals as roughly good or roughly bad across all categories of measurement.

For example, research by Romano and Bordieri found that professors who are considered physically attractive by students are considered to be better teachers than unattractive professors. Attractive professors are also more likely to be asked for help on problems. These same attractive professors also tend to receive positive recommendations from students and are less likely to receive the blame when a student receives a failing grade.

Perceptions of attractiveness also influence competence ratings in the workplace. An MSNBC survey described in the article "Power of Attraction still rules in workplace," notes that:

Good looks appeared significant to both men and women and the workplace. About 58 percent of female bosses who were rated as attractive got high marks for competence, compared with 41 percent of "average-looking" female bosses and only 23 percent of unattractive supervisors. Among people with male bosses, 61 percent who rated their supervisors as good-looking also found them competent, compared with 41 percent for the average types and 25 percent for those rated unattractive.

As you would expect, the reverse is also true. People judged to have a single undesirable trait are also judged to possess many poor or negative traits, even though there was no evidence to support such a judgment. The conclusion is that a single negative trait will become generalized.

The bottom line for us is important: first impressions are critical. Attractiveness comes down to a first impression that triggers other impressions. You can go a long way towards inheriting other positive impressions by improving the perception of your attractiveness.

Attractiveness Leads to Likeability and Credibility

As you've just seen, attractiveness is important, even vital. How is it relevant to our discussion of Credibility and Likeability, and is it realistic to expect that we can make an appreciable change in our looks or overall attractiveness? Let's take each question separately.

How is attractiveness related to Likeability and Credibility? Simple. The more attractive the person, the more likely he or she is to be perceived as trustworthy, likeable and competent. They come in a set.

Robert Cialdini in the *Psychology of Persuasion* says that we are more apt to like a physically attractive person, and more likely to help a physically attractive person. Other studies referenced by Eddy Elmer suggest that we are more likely to confide in an attractive person, and the more we open up to someone, the more likely we are to trust and like that person.

Bottom line, one of the keys to improving your trust, Likeability and Credibility is to improve your attractiveness. In this way, you can take advantage of the psychology that will run on autopilot from the first impression.

Can you make a measurable difference in your attractiveness? Yes! Although you can't dramatically change the structure of your face (without extensive cosmetic surgery), there are multiple things you can do to make yourself appear more attractive. There's that word *appear* again. Remember, what we're dealing with are first impressions and perceptions. It's all about the perception of your attractiveness. There are many subtle things you can do to increase the perception of attractiveness and thereby improve the perception of your Credibility and Likeability. When you look at those *before and after* photos on the makeover shows, you can see how simple *style* changes can drastically improve appearance.

What Influences the Perception of Attractiveness?

The Universal Look

We found far too much research on this topic to cite all the sources, but most of the findings are the same. The consensus is that most cultures perceive several qualities or characteristics as attractive or beautiful. Research collected by Eddy Elmer and Jim Houran and published in their article "Physical Attractiveness in the Workplace" sums up the findings that there is a universally attractive *look*. We find that the characteristics of this Universal Look include:

- *Symmetrical face.* Slight imperfections are typically expected, but more severe ones become problematic. Those would include out-of-proportion features: a crooked nose, eyes that are mismatched, a nose that is too large or too small or a lopsided mouth.

- *Symmetrical body.*

- *Clear skin and vibrant hair.*

- *Full lips with straight and white teeth.*

- *For men:* square jaw, wide shoulders, defined chest and strong arms (features that indicate the man is healthy and a good protector).

- *For women:* full red lips, large breasts, strong hips, voluptuous buttocks (features that indicate the woman would make a good mate and child bearer).

- *For both men and women, but especially for men:* Features associated with a baby's face are deemed attractive.

The Magic Number

In the list above, we mentioned "symmetrical face and body." There is much more here than just a triangular or pear shape. In fact, there is a "magic number" that is almost universally accepted as the key to beauty. The number was published in 1202 by Leonardo of Pisa (called "Fibonacci") in his book on mathematics *Liber Abaci*. Throughout history, painters, musicians, sculptors, architects and mathematicians have explored this magic number. For our purposes, we simply share it with you to let you know that perceptions of beauty are not necessarily subjective; rather they are predictable by centuries of quantitative science. If your own proportions are off from the Golden Number, you might seek to change them, if possible, especially if attractiveness is important to you.

The Golden Ratio in the Human Body

The *ideal* proportion is 1.618. If you were to take measurements of an average human body, you'd find that number recurring many times. A few of those occurrences are:

- The distance between the finger tip and the elbow / distance between the wrist and the elbow

- The distance between the shoulder line and the top of the head / head length

- The distance between the navel and the top of the head / the distance between the shoulder line and the top of the head

- The distance between the navel and knee / distance between the knee and the end of the foot

The Golden Ratio in the Human Face

There are several golden ratios in the human face. For example, the total width of the two front teeth over their height gives a golden ratio. The width of the first tooth from the centre to the second tooth is also a golden ratio. Some other golden ratios in the human face are:

- Length of face / width of face

- Distance between the lips and where the eyebrows meet / length of nose

- Length of face / distance between tip of jaw and where the eyebrows meet

- Length of mouth / width of nose

- Width of nose / distance between nostrils

- Distance between pupils / distance between eyebrows

Our purpose here is simply to inform you that other people will perceive you as attractive (or not) based on this Magic Number, the ratio of attractiveness.

More than Physical

We've talked about the physical attributes, but what about the psychological attributes that influence our perception of attractiveness?

Elmer and Houran in "Physical Attractiveness in the Workplace" note that a person's body image, including the level of comfort with his or her own body, influences attractiveness. The point is, even beautiful people can be seen as less attractive when they do not like their bodies or feel uncomfortable in them. In fact, a physically unattractive person's comfort with how he looks can sometimes make up for physical flaws, and thereby make him more attractive.

Style trumps magic. A person's style—as demonstrated by posture, stature, gait, eye contact and smile—can impact the perception of attractiveness. Some people have a smile that is warm or bright enough to accentuate average physical features or even offset particularly unattractive ones. Step in front of the mirror and take a critical look at your smile. If you don't like what you see, figure out what to do to change it.

We know from experience that there are many people we consider attractive who don't fit the basic model of attractiveness. If you were to look at their features individually, you would conclude that they are not all that attractive. However, they come across with something extra that makes them seem more attractive. What is that something extra? Could it be charisma?

In our research into charisma, we've discovered that the perception of charisma is directly related to the amount of focus given to the other person. In other words, if you want to be seen as charismatic, you need to focus directly on the other person as though he or she is the most fascinating person you've ever met. Your rapport-building skills are directly linked to your charisma, which is directly linked to your attractiveness.

Leveraging Familiarity

Another interesting finding about attractiveness is in the area of familiarity and similarity. It appears that the more familiar someone is to us, the more attractive we are likely to view him or her. The more similar the person is to us, the more attractive he or she will appear to us.

How does this work? When we find people attractive, they are able to bypass some of our internal filters. We see them as more familiar and therefore safer, and we are more likely to want to interact with them. The more we interact, the more attractive they become and the more we like them. It's a self-perpetuating process.

Sometimes it is as simple as proximity. Research shows that people who are in close proximity to us are more physically attractive to us. Work by Robert Zajonc suggests that merely being in the general vicinity of another person will increase our liking for that person, and the longer two people are in close proximity, the greater the chance they will end up liking each other.

Similarity is another aspect of attractiveness. People who are similar to us (in terms of looks, personal characteristics and attitude) are seen as more physically attractive. We trust, find attractive and like people who are *like us* both on the inside and the outside.

The bottom line is, we find attractive and like people who are similar and familiar to us. Therefore, we can influence the perception of attractiveness simply by accentuating similarities, increasing familiarity and maximizing exposure. But it's not just any old exposure that is important; it's meaningful exposure. Research by Donald Dutton found, "People with whom we have experienced something emotional or physically arousing are perceived as more attractive after the event than before the event."

Chapter 5:
What Is Likeability?

Likeability is an illusive quality. It's not what it seems. Of the people you have ever known, you like some and dislike others. That's a given in anyone's life. The point is, few people can pinpoint what causes one person to like another person. Which characteristic tips the scale? Could you name the decision criteria you use to tag someone with the *liked* label? If you ask Bob, "Why do you like John?" you're likely to get a dumbfounded look and a response like "Ur, well, uh, he's funny, he's nice, he's a good guy," or some other vague answer. Conversely, you probably find it impossible to pinpoint what it is about yourself that makes you likeable or not likeable.

The research has shown that Likeability is important to success. In fact, it rivals Credibility in its importance. We see evidence of this every day. For example, in the 2008 Democratic primaries, Hillary Clinton showed herself to be competent and credible. No one questioned her *commander-in-chief-ness*, but there was some quality missing. That something was Likeability. In an article in the *Wall Street Journal (June 4, 2008)*, Clinton's former Campaign Manager Patti Doyle said, "Emphasizing experience over Likeability may have been her 'fatal flaw.'"

Likeability Characteristics. We know Likeability is important, and we know it when we see it, but what exactly is it? Our research shows that Likeability is a combination of characteristics including (but not limited to) interest, empathy and genuineness. In a professional context, likeable people tend to be interesting to us, interested in us, empathetic, positive, non-judgmental and genuine. Is simply having likeable qualities enough to make you likeable? No.

The Likeability disclaimer. Those characteristics are like any other characteristic—measured in percentages. No one is 100 percent any characteristic, as that would indicate an obsession. For example, someone who is extremely interested in you is commonly called a stalker. Someone who is extremely empathetic is often considered codependent, and a person who is extremely positive may be viewed as naive. Because no one is 100 percent of those characteristics, this means each of us represents a different combination of percentages.

How much is enough for someone to like you? It depends entirely on the criteria that the other person uses to determine Likeability. That's because Likeability is an impression—a subconscious perception. In other words, your Likeability is the result of the other person's unconscious mental activity processing the data related to your Likeability Characteristics. Conversely, you will use your intuition to calculate the varying levels of those characteristics for each person you encounter. You put data into your mind at one end, and an impression comes out at the other end.

For example, the data that represents me has to satisfy your criteria for Likeability, otherwise you will find me lacking in Likeability. When I meet your criteria, you will find yourself drawn to me. With that in mind, the more you know about the different characteristics and principles of Likeability, the better able you will be to make yourself more likeable to more people.

The Principles of Likeability

Let's look at Likeability in a different way. In addition to the characteristics, there are several Principles of Likeability. They are:

- We like people who are familiar to us in some way (Familiarity).

- We like people who are similar to us in some way (Similarity).

- We like people who are genuinely interested in our concerns and values (Interest).

- We like people who make themselves easy to like in return (trustworthy, positive, non-judgmental, real).

Subconscious Likeability Scorecard

How do we calculate the different Likeability Characteristics and Principles to determine whether someone is likeable? We subconsciously keep a Likeability Scorecard in our heads, and we add points or subtract points as we get to know a person.

Is he:

- Friendly?

- Interesting to me?

- Interested in me?

- Familiar?

- Similar?

That is the first round of attributes. Once past them, we then begin to notice (and score) additional attitude elements:

- Positive and upbeat (add a point) or negative and whiney (subtract a point)?

- Accepting and open (add a point) or close-minded and judgmental (subtract a point)?

- Real, human, and vulnerable (add a point) or robotic, unemotional, and arrogant (subtract a point)?

Familiarity and Similarity—
The Common Denominators

We humans tend to get uncomfortable around people who are different from us. Another way to look at that is, we are attracted to people we find familiar and/or similar—similar both on the inside in terms of experiences, values and beliefs and similar on the outside. Let's take a look at some of the research that substantiates this statement.

Familiarity: More Exposure Breeds Likeability

The more familiar the person, the more apt we are to like him. Research conducted by Bailenson, Iyengar, and Yee at Stanford University shows that we respond positively to political candidates who look familiar to us. The Stanford team morphed pictures of familiar faces (Hillary Clinton & John McCain in this case) with unfamiliar faces and found the more familiar the face, the more favorable the response.

We know from research conducted in the sixties by Robert Zajonc that the mere exposure to a person is sufficient to increase the Likeability of that person. This is known as the *Exposure Effect* (also known as the *Mere Exposure Effect*). It is a psychological principle that says that people express undue liking for things merely because they are familiar with them. This effect has been nicknamed the *familiarity breeds liking* effect.

We see this regularly play out in advertising and media campaigns. A political party with deep pockets has a better chance of winning an election simply because it can afford to increase exposure to its messages and candidates. The same is true of corporations with hefty advertising budgets. It is how brands are traditionally established.

Repetition can certainly strengthen a message and increase Likeability, but it can also reach the point of diminishing returns. Too much exposure, or more precisely, too much repetition of the same message can actually lessen Likeability. Have you ever noticed that a TV spot that makes you laugh the first time you see it will cause you to retch after repeated viewings? The solution in marketing is to create a strategy that presents variations on the theme. The solution in sales or politics is to make sure you're not one-dimensional. The more interests you share with the person you want to connect with, the more likeable you can become.

Similarity: We Like People Who Are Like Us

This may sound overly simplistic, but we like people who are like us. That means people who are similar to us on the inside and on the outside. As humans, we are compelled to find points of similarity. We look for and are attracted to people who are like us in terms of values, interests and experiences.

Looks like me. Sounds like me.

Albeit a tad bit creepy, research shows that we are attracted to people who physically look like us. It appears there is an aspect of our human nature that has us constantly seeking points of similarity to ourselves. Dr. Karen Stephenson describes it as "an ancient skill encoded in us by our forebears."

> "In the small talk of cocktail parties, humans are at random walk, desperately seeking points of similarity

through visibility: height, girth, dress, gender, race, accent, hair and eye color, etc. Reading the audience and working a room are ancient skills encoded in us by our forebears who sat cheek by jowl around the campfire; an earlier and more primordial form of cocktail party. I confess to having attended countless cocktail parties and continue to be amazed how, after just a few drinks, I end up with people who are like me in some way— same experiences, same clothes, same interests, etc. It's not the alcohol talking, but the ancient drive of seeking similarity: 'You look like me, you think like me, you dress like me ... you're one of us.' When people connect at this basic level, they are engaging in an embryonic form of trust with each other. What began as a room full of disconnected people may end up as a network of people connected in invisible lines of trust."

As a fun illustration, take a look at the following two photos. In 1999, I (PH) found Dr. Karen Stephenson's articles on the web quite by accident. I connected with her work and her words immediately. It wasn't until much later that I noticed the physical similarities. Take a look at Figure 5-1. That's Dr. Karen on the right and me on the left (what we looked like at the time).

Figure 5-1 – Holloway and Stephenson

We like political candidates who look like us

Stanford researchers Bailenson, Iyengar, and Yee performed two studies on facial similarity: one in 2004 and a second in 2007. In the initial study, conducted one week before the 2004 election, a representative sample of voters viewed images of George Bush and John Kerry morphed with their own image. The results showed that those who were strongly partisan were unmoved by facial similarity manipulation, but the less rigid partisans and independents preferred the candidate with whom their own face had been morphed. Figure 5-2 shows a subtle example of this morphing.

Subject   George Bush   Morph
(35% Subject, 65% Bush)

Figure 5-2: Face Morphed with George W. Bush
Photos by Nick Yee

In the follow-up study, the Stanford team compared the effects of policy and facial similarity using a set of prospective 2008 presidential candidates. Even though the effects of party and policy similarity dominated, facial similarity proved a significant cue for unfamiliar and same-gender candidates. An illustration from the study is shown in figure 5-3.

Subject	Hillary Clinton	Morph
		(35% Subject, 65% Clinton)

Figure 5-3: Face Morphed with Hillary Clinton
Photos by Nick Yee

The point is, facial similarity plays an important part in our decision making. We tend to like people who look like us. We tend to respond to people who look like us, too. In the Stanford research, voters preferred candidates who resembled them in appearance. "You are more likely to support the candidate who most resembles you in a nonverbal sense, especially if you don't know much about the candidate's platform," said Shanto Iyengar, professor of political science and communications at Stanford University.

So how can you use this in the real world? Seek to look similar to the people with whom you want to connect. What if your face is not similar to your prospect's? The answer is so obvious that very few people can see it: focus on the other person's facial expressions, because the psychology of similarity extends to facial expressions.

In other words, when you encounter someone who makes the same facial expressions as you do, you will perceive that person as similar to yourself. The lines on your face are a map of the facial expressions you've made over your lifetime. Thus, they are a reflection of who you are on the inside, and other people recognize it subconsciously.

Shares my values, beliefs, interests and experiences

We are attracted to and like people who share our values, beliefs, interests and experiences. We see examples of this often in the political realm. We vote for the candidate who is most like us, the candidate we can relate to, the candidate who shares our interests and experiences (military service, volunteer work, the generation we grew up in, our ideas, dreams and passions, for example).

While this is not a book on politics, it is our contention that the success of most political candidates is directly related to the extent they are like their constituents. The highest form of *alikeness* is sharing values and beliefs. If I feel you share my values and beliefs, I am much more likely to trust you and like you.

Likeable Qualities

We like people who make themselves easy to like. How do you do that? You should be:

- Friendly and empathetic
- Interesting/Interested in me
- Upbeat and positive
- Open and non-judgmental
- Real, human, vulnerable

We Like People Who Are Friendly and Empathetic

One of the principles of Likeability is that we like people who like us. We demonstrate this *liking* through friendliness and empathy. We are open and responsive, warm and welcoming and we show this in our face, demeanor and words.

We Like People Who Are Interesting *to* Us and Interested *in* Us

Likeable people spark interest. Interest is a two-pronged element. We like people who are interesting *to* us and people who are interested *in* us. Both are important, but *interested in me* usually wins out. Dale Carnegie wrote, "You can make more friends in two months by becoming interested in other people than you can in two years by trying to get other people interested in you."

Author Jay Conger, in the *Harvard Business Review* article, "The Necessary Art of Persuasion," says, "If we believe someone has a sincere interest in our concerns, we are naturally receptive to their messages."

We like people who are sincerely and genuinely interested in us. This is a critically important element of Likeability, and something you can actually do something about. If you want to become more likeable, simply hone your *interested in* skills. How would you show someone that you were interested in him or her?

We Like People Who Are Upbeat and Positive

Likeable people are also upbeat and positive. Daniel Goleman, Richard Boyantzis, and Annie McKee, authors of *Primal Leadership*, note that "people who have the ability to exude upbeat feelings are emotional magnets for others." We simply like being around them. "Emotional leaders have a knack for acting as a limbic 'attractor,' exerting a palpable force on the emotional brains of people around them."

Developing a more positive attitude does not mean ignoring hardships or failures. It is simply reframing those difficulties and negative emotions to healthier positive ones. The old cliché, "When life gives you lemons, make lemonade," has been around for a while because it is exactly the winning attitude that people are attracted to, and it is exactly the attitude which brings rewards.

Essential to be both empathetic and uplifting

It's important to be both empathetic and uplifting. If you're only empathetic and you're empathetic to people who are depressed, in despair, or otherwise stuck in some negative space, you won't be very likeable, even to those in a similar mental state.

We like people who offer us hope and show us the path forward out of our problems. In politics, think of the power of John Kennedy's rousing "Dare to Dream" speech. Compare this to Jimmy Carter's 1979 "Crisis of Confidence" speech.

In the summer of 1979, advisors told President Carter that Americans were suffering from a general *crisis of confidence* and needed inspiration. A well-intentioned Carter withdrew to Camp David to sit down with Americans from all walks of life to understand what was bothering them.

He listened and empathized, perhaps a bit too much. On the evening of July 15, 1979, he delivered what was perhaps the most important speech of his presidency. Carter talked about the sessions at Camp David. He urged Americans to conserve energy. "The solution of our energy crisis can also help us to conquer the crisis of the spirit in our country," the president said, asking Americans to join him in adapting to a new age of limits.

But he also admonished them, "In a nation proud of hard work, strong families, close-knit communities and our faith in God, too many of us now tend to worship self-indulgence and consumption. Human identity is no longer defined by what one does but by what one owns."

Although the American public seemed to appreciate his frankness, the speech was perceived as neither positive nor uplifting. In the PBS Special, *The American Experience – Jimmy Carter*, Historian Roger Wilkins notes that the problem was with Carter himself. "When your leadership is demonstrably weaker than it should be, you don't then point at the people and say, 'It's your problem.' If you want the people to move, you move them the way Roosevelt moved them, or you exhort them the way Kennedy or Johnson exhorted them. You don't say, 'It's your fault.'"

Author Frank Luntz, in *Words that Work*, describes it this way:

> "It was a litany of despair and defeat that Americans had never heard from their president until that night. And while he took some responsibility, the message heard by the American people was that it was America's fault. The speech was a reminder not of what Americans could be if they dared to dream, but rather a declaration of what they had in fact become. Instead of appealing to American aspirations, the malaise speech harped on their anxieties and insecurities."

We Like People Who Are Open and Non-judgmental

The truly likeable are nonjudgmental. They recognize the difference between judging ideas or opinions versus judging the people who espouse those ideas and opinions. The truly likeable treat everyone with respect and understanding regardless of their baggage.

Likeable people are flexible and open to new people, ideas, and ways of doing things. They demonstrate their openness in their behavior, the tone of their voice, their facial expressions and their language.

Take a look at the two faces in Figure 5-4. Which one are you more likely to respond positively to?

Figure 5-4: Which face is more likeable?

The face on the left is a judging face. The face on the right is much more open. We purposely used the same woman for both photos to show that even those whose natural response is *judging* can learn to control the results of that mental process so that the face looks a little more inviting. This is a simple change to make. Just identify the face you want people to see when they encounter you, then begin to wear it throughout the day. You will discover an interesting phenomenon—your mental state follows your facial expression.

We Like People Who Are Real, Human and Vulnerable

We like people who are real, people who aren't afraid to make mistakes, people who overcome challenges, people who show their soft side. For example, Americans watched Hillary Clinton crying at a coffee shop in New Hampshire during the 2008 presidential primary. Although some consider it emotional blackmail, anecdotal evidence suggests that when Hillary showed some emotion, it actually helped her campaign rather than hurt it. Here's the story as reported by ABC News:

Clinton was sitting at a table in a café in Portsmouth, New Hampshire with 16 undecided voters, mostly women, warmly and calmly taking questions. Then she took an unexpected question from a woman standing in the back.

"My question is very personal, how do you do it?" asked Marianne Pernold Young, a freelance photographer from Portsmouth, New Hampshire. She mentioned Clinton's hair and appearance always looking perfectly coifed. "How do you, how do you keep upbeat and so wonderful?"

Hillary responded with:

"You know, I think, well luckily, on special days I do have help. If you see me every day and if you look on some of the websites and listen to some of the commentators they always find me on the day I didn't have help. It's not easy. It's not easy, and I couldn't do it if I didn't passionately believe it was the right thing to do. You know, I have so many opportunities from this country and just don't want to see us fall backwards.

(Eyes welling up a bit) You know, this is very personal for me. It's not just political it's not just public. I see what's happening, and we have to reverse it. Some people think elections are a game, lot's of who's up or who's down, [but] it's about our country, it's about our kids' futures, and it's really about all of us together."

It wasn't so much what Senator Clinton said that had impact—it was the show of emotion connected to those words. After the event, Pernold Young told ABC News that she was glad Clinton showed emotion. "She allowed herself to feel," Pernold Young said. "I was surprised and I said, 'Wow there's someone there.'"

Although Pernold Young appreciated the brief glimpse into the real Hillary, apparently it didn't last long enough. In the end she voted for Obama. Pernold Young said while she was moved by Clinton's emotional moment, she was turned off by how quickly the New York senator regained her "political posture."

"I went to see Hillary. I was undecided and I was moved by her response to me. We saw 10 seconds of Hillary, the caring woman. But then when she turned away from me, I noticed that she stiffened up and took on that political posture again," she said. "And the woman that I noticed for 10 seconds was gone."

It's not what you do; it's who you are that matters. It's not just a moment here and there of genuineness that's important. To have a positive effect on your Likeability, that genuineness must be a real, natural and consistent part of who you are every day.

The Likeability Effect in U.S. Presidential Campaigns

As a testament to the power of Likeability, consider that Americans have never elected a president they didn't like, with the possible exception of Richard Nixon.

Regardless of how you might feel about George W. Bush's competence, most would give him high marks for Likeability. We are convinced this is why he won in 2000 and 2004. Compare Bush's Likeability with that of John Kerry. John Kerry was clearly more competent than Bush, but something about him just didn't sit right with many voters. Where Bush did well in the *is like me* and *likes me* categories, Kerry scored low on both. He came across as elitist and arrogant. You got the sense that he felt he was better than you.

The same was said of Hillary Clinton. Words used to describe her include cold, arrogant and egotistical. What was the impact? In June of 2007, Clinton was the front-runner in the Democratic primary but ranked third in Likeability behind Obama and John Edwards. It's all history now; her competence was trumped by her lack of Likeability.

An important aspect of Likeability is the ability to *connect*. Republican vice presidential candidate Sarah Palin scored high in Likeability because she connected with a large cross-section of *regular* Americans. Compare Palin's Likeability to Hillary Clinton's Likeability. In an article by Jeanna Bryner titled "Marketing the Next President of the United States," University of British Columbia researchers Lewis and Hoegg tell us:

"Hillary Clinton struggles in terms of making connections. Barack Obama tends to be more fluid and much more likeable. So despite the enormous advantages that Hillary had coming into this, in terms of fundraising, in terms of awareness, this likeability deficit explains how well Obama is doing."

Later in the 2008 election, we watched as McCain and Obama debated on national television. While pollsters and pundits scored the debates in terms of party lines and debate points, we scored the candidates on Likeability and Credibility. We rank the candidates relatively close in terms of Credibility, but give Obama higher scores for Likeability. Overall we gave the *wins* to Obama but ranked McCain a very close second.

The majority of post-debate polls showed the two candidates relatively close in terms of who won the debate, with Obama having a moderate edge. The CNN Likeability poll was a different story. It gave Obama an appreciable *Likeability* lead over McCain.

Newsweek's Andrew Romano also writes about the importance of likeability, observing that in 1984 Reagan struck voters as about 20 percent more likeable than Mondale. Bush senior defeated Dukakis largely because he triumphed in the congeniality competition and later lost to Clinton largely because he didn't.

After the October 17, 2000, debate, voters rated Bush junior as the more likeable candidate by a margin of 60–30; four years later, he whipped Kerry 52–41 in the same department. In other words, the candidate who won the debates may not have won the subsequent election, but the candidate who won the Likeability contest almost always did.

Romano adds that all of this bodes well for Obama. "According to the CNN poll, viewers found the Illinois Democrat more likeable last night by a margin of 65 to 28 percent—a far larger spread than either Reagan, Bush, Clinton or W. ever enjoyed in similar surveys."

Why Is It Important that We Like Our President?

When Hillary was taking a lot of flak about her lack of Likeability, many people questioned whether Likeability ought to be a factor at all. CNN.com writer Bill Schneider discussed this with Stephen Hess, a presidential historian at the Brookings Institute in Washington DC. Hess notes, "If you were listing the things a president had to be good at, like being commander-in-chief or being chief executive of a federal bureaucracy, you wouldn't put likeability up there as a necessary quality." That's an interesting comment from a guy who used to work in the Eisenhower administration, which had the winning campaign slogan "I like Ike."

Hess suggested that when people choose a president, it's like hiring someone for a job. The first thing voters want to know is, "Can the candidate do the job?" We agree with the belief that the ability to do the job ought to be the first and maybe the only consideration for whom we elect as President. The reality is, however, that Americans are simply not wired that way. We seem to want to vote for someone we actually like. A writer for the online magazine *Insight* describes it this way:

> Americans, after all, don't just elect a resume—they elect a person. They know that the person they choose will not only make key decisions but will be on their television screens, and thus in their living room and kitchen, for the next four years. They therefore have to like the person they elect.

> And more than just liking a candidate, Americans often feel the need to romanticize or create myths about their presidents. They don't just want to pull a lever on Election Day; their patriotism cries out for more. Americans want to feel as though they have a personal relationship with their leaders. Foreigners have never been able to grasp this aspect of the American psyche: Americans have to feel something in their heart and soul for the person they choose. In short, Americans love to fall in love with their presidents. They see it as synonymous with loving their nation.

Chapter 6:
How to Become More Likeable

This chapter is deceptively important. It's perhaps the most important in the book. This is where you can see in black and white the many different ways you can either make the case for your Likeability or destroy it. As well-worn as the following bit of advice sounds, it is more important than ever in today's skeptical world: everything you say and do tells people something about you. In fact, everything you don't do says just as much about you too. Every facial expression you do not make, every gesture you do not make, every concept you do not explain—they all display the quality of your thinking and decisions, which displays the depth of your values. Now, let's look at the details.

1. Look the Part

In the Trust chapter we looked at how your face and demeanor contribute to the perception of trustworthiness. The same is true for Likeability, and many of the same elements are at play. A likeable look is open, warm and welcoming. The posture is open, and smiles are genuinely expressed through the eyes.

Making small changes. We explained earlier that people with baby-face features are often viewed as more likeable, while those with a mature face are perceived as more credible. Our coaching clients ask us if it is possible to alter the *look* of your face to give the effect of either. Yes, it is.

If you want to appear more likeable, modify your look to give yourself a more rounded, smiling face. When you want to look more credible, shift to a more elongated, serious face. Simply opening or closing your mouth a little can make a huge change one way or the other.

Change expression. Although you obviously can't change the physical shape of your face or your bone structure, you actually can change the appearance of your face dramatically simply by changing your expression. If you have a more credible but not so likeable look, simply learn to smile from your heart. What does that mean? It means a genuine smile that shows up across your face and in particular in your eyes. It also causes your cheeks to puff up a bit, showing a more rounded jaw line.

Hair do and don't. For men, adding a goatee or other beard to your chin will add length to your face. Conversely, shaving the beard off will give you a rounder face. Facial hair in general works to *mature* the face, so if you're trying to improve the Likeability look, you may want to lose the facial hair.

An interesting research study by Reed and Blunk looked at the influence of facial hair on impression formation. In particular, researchers measured the perception of job applicants for managerial positions and found consistently more positive perceptions of attractiveness, personality, competency and composure for men with facial hair.

That study underscores the impact of context on perception. Subjects were looking for management material. Although Likeability would certainly be a factor, my guess is that the other factors played a more prominent role. Those factors would be competence, personality (which in this case was dominance) and attractiveness/charisma.

A second study led by Hellstrom and Tekle at Stockholm University looked at the effects of glasses, hair and beard on judgments of occupation and personal qualities. They found that participants associated glasses with intellectualism and goodness, being bald with idealism, and beards with unconventionality and goodness.

Most people add facial hair as a form of self-expression. Most people choose glasses based on style. Most people choose hair style as a form of self-expression. Our advice is to take a long, hard look at yourself in a mirror. Is that the image that serves you best for what you want to accomplish? If not, do something about it.

2. Speak the Language

As in all aspects of Likeability, the key to sounding likeable is to sound like the person you're talking with. This is a very basic psychological concept that was popularized first by Carl Rogers. He wrote, "The best vantage point for understanding behavior is from the internal frame of reference of the individual." In other words, to understand and connect with someone else, do it from their perspective.

It's commonly thought that a likeable voice is calm and soothing. That's only true if the person you're talking with has a calm, soothing voice. Ever find yourself in a hurry and need to get information from someone who is calm and soothing? That's a recipe for disaster.

In order to entice someone into liking you, it's important to match how that person talks. Here is your scorecard:

Volume	
Speed	
Pitch	
Modulation	
Dialect	
Energy	

If you simply pay attention to those elements in how the other person talks, you'll know what adjustments to make. Your goal is to approximate how the other person talks. The closer you come to sounding like that person, the easier it becomes for that person to like you.

The Language of Likeability

As president, George W. Bush created a great amount of media commentary on his tendency to butcher the English language. His syntax and grammar are often a mess. He has trouble pronouncing the names of international leaders and places and seems incapable of completing an off-the-cuff thought, but he gets away with it because he makes his meaning clear. That was exactly George Orwell's point when he said "The defense of the English language has nothing to do with correct grammar or syntax, which is of no importance so long as one makes one's meaning clear."

For those who can't fathom why Bush won the presidency, here's how political pollster Frank Luntz explains it: "He succeeded against opponents who were arguably intellectually his superior precisely because voters knew exactly where he stood."

What is likeable language?

Likeable language is informal, upbeat and positive. It is action focused, jargon free and to the point. It is real, heartfelt and contains references to real people, real struggles and actual accomplishments. It is honest without being demoralizing, and it is hopeful.

Likeable language is simple and straightforward. George Orwell's language rules continue to be relevant:

- Never use a metaphor, simile or other figure of speech that you are used to seeing in print.

- Never use a long word when a short one will do.

- If it is possible to cut a word out, always cut a word out.

- Never use a passive when you can use an active.

- Never use a foreign phrase, a scientific word, or a jargon word if you can think of an everyday English equivalent.

Pam and I have developed a few of our own rules:

- Always match the vocal nonverbals of the other person.

- Always move the conversation forward.

- Always engage the other person with verbal and nonverbal questions.

- Always give the other person room to change his mind.

- Always listen actively because that is the most important part of your participation in any conversation.

Look into my Words...

Leo Burnett, a famous advertising guru, is recognized for having analyzed both advertisements and timeless documents to see what made them work or fail. The result is the rule that verbs always trump adjectives, and some advice - a rough ratio of verbs to adjectives. Simply, the more adjectives, the worse the motivational power.

The Declaration of Independence, for example, contains only 11.7% adjectives, the Gettysburg Address, 13.1 percent adjectives. Winston Churchill's famous "Blood, Sweat, and Tears" speech contains 12.1% adjectives. A similar percentage of adjectives is found in The Lord's Prayer, the Ten Commandments, as well as the Preamble to the U.S. Constitution.

What do all these communications have in common? They inspire, they persuade, they call to action. In order to accomplish this, they are heavy on verbs and light on adjectives. In my (ML) study of psychology and clinical practice, I learned very early on that the mind follows positively phrased, action verbs. Those are the simple directions that cause the mind to take action. Adjectives are meaningless in the act of inspiring, influencing and motivating people to take action.

Here's the point. To make your language more likeable, use fewer adjectives and more appropriate verbs. Our research, training and experience continue to prove that connecting with someone and making yourself likeable is the result of your conscious mind tapping into someone else's subconscious mind. As John Grinder, co-developer of Neuro-Linguistic Programming, said, "In the subconscious mind, there are no nouns—only verbs."

3. Demonstrate Genuine Interest

Here's a tool that will help you communicate your interest to the person you're talking to. It's really pretty simple: just imagine that the other person is the most fascinating person you've met lately.

Go into your bathroom, turn on the lights, and lock the door behind you. Now remember, the face in the mirror is you, so as you're standing there imagine you're someone else looking at you. Put on the most sincere and likeable facial expression you can muster. Would you like that face? Now, put on the most serious and credible face you have. Would you trust or like that face? Next, begin to tell a story (out loud) and watch your facial expressions—or lack of expressions. Would you like that face? Finally, start over and tell that story as though you're talking to the most fascinating person you've ever met. Are you believable?

Many years ago, I (ML) was asked to audition as the spokesperson for a new radio station. I was told to deliver a short promotional script in different styles—friendly and sexy. I started with the sexy style, but when I finished, the casting director said, "OK, that's enough for the friendly style. Now let's see how sexy you can be." Obviously, the answer was—not very!

The point is, many of us do not know what we look like when we're talking to other people. The more you know about how the other person experiences you, the more effective you can be at adapting your style and improving how people experience you.

4. Listen Empathetically

In his classic, *The Seven Habits of Highly Effective Leaders*, Stephen Covey makes the following observation: "Most people do not listen with the intent to understand; they listen with the intent to reply."

Our own experience with coaching professionals is that many of them don't even hear the message the other person is transmitting. They hear their own internal dialog.

In a world in which so many people have so much trouble actually listening to other people, a person who has developed excellent listening skills is magnetic. Covey refers to this type of listening as *empathic*. We might think of empathic listening as turning up the hearing aid. It involves listening carefully enough to identify the emotion behind a message as well as the content of the message.

While some people are naturally more empathetic than others, listening skills can be improved. It has been our experience that they can be improved dramatically and immediately. The key is to heap great value and Credibility onto the other person. Listen from his or her perspective and assume that you do not want to miss anything he or she has to say. Isn't that the way you would listen if you were talking with one of your heroes? To practice empathic listening:

- Pause before you respond.
- Verify your understanding of the message.
- Make a statement in concert with what you heard.
- Ask a question about the other person's perspective.
- Demonstrate respect for the concerns you hear—whether you agree with those concerns or not.

5. Be Congruent

Your Likeability is determined in large measure by *how* you communicate. Your Credibility is determined by your congruence in terms of how you feel about *what* you communicate. Luckily, scientists seek to determine the elements of communication and the value of each element. The most famous findings come from Albert Mehrabian, (Professor Emeritus of Psychology, UCLA). He identified three elements of a face-to-face communication and calculated the value of each. The numbers below show you how important each element is to your Likeability:

- Words: 7%

- Tone and voice: 38%

- Body language: 55%

It is perfectly possible for me to disagree with all of your content (words) and still like you. In modern history, George W. Bush seems to embody this idea. A highly polarizing politician, more people like him than agree with him.

Chances are, you're not dealing with global terrorism and nuclear war, so you have a better chance of making it possible for people to like your content as well as to like you. What makes it possible? When your voice and your body are in agreement with what you say, it becomes possible. Of course, it helps if the message is one that benefits the other person.

Here is an example of how the formula above works. First, in order for you to get the maximum value from them, you have to be speaking about feelings or emotions. Let's say you are talking about a specific problem the other person faces. You say, "I'm sorry this situation is having this affect on you." If your voice and body are congruent with your words, then you score 100 percent. Let's say you are looking out the window or brushing lint off your coat when you deliver those words. Your score would drop considerably. You would be showing yourself as incongruent because your body language did not match your words.

In a different context, if you're making a presentation of factual data, the formula would not be relevant until you began to discuss how you felt about the data. "Gentlemen, the facts are in front of you. I'm afraid we have some tough choices to make that will hurt every one of us." Again, if your voice and body language do not match your words, your Likeability score will drop.

In order to understand what this incongruence looks like, let's look at a failed political commercial. It was one of John Kerry's very first in the 2004 presidential race. In the commercial, he talks about a spirit of optimism and hope. His wife, Teresa Heinz-Kerry, talks about these concepts as well. As alluring as the concepts are, however, both the candidate and his wife show nonverbal language that contradicts their beautiful words. The conflict is created through the mismatch between their words and their facial expressions. Drew Weston thought the commercial important enough to discuss it in his book *The Political Brain*. He describes it this way:

> Teresa Heinz-Kerry introduces the theme of optimism with an incongruent facial expression – a mixture of serious and dour—that undercut the words. Then the senator reiterated the theme, with his facial expression similarly discordant from the language. His face was flat and impassive—no smile, no twinkle, nothing to engender feelings of excitement, national pride or hope. The optimism theme seemed grafted onto both the message and the candidate.

The point here is that your face and the sound of your words must be congruent with the words themselves in order for people listening to trust and believe you.

6. Judge Without Being Judgmental

There is a big difference between judging and being judgmental. Let's look closely at both concepts:

- Judging is the act of surveying and evaluating data objectively, with no emotional involvement. This is how we determine the viability of something new to us.

  - Annuities are appropriate in certain situations.

  - Some real estate agents provide an excellent service.

  - Many corporations are ethical.

  - The health care system could use some help.

- Being judgmental is a subjective (or opinionated) critique based on your personal beliefs of what is right or appropriate. It is generalizing or packaging personal beliefs, then applying them as global criteria. This is how we develop illogical and negative, universal beliefs, such as:

  - All Democrats are liberal.

  - All Republicans are warmongers.

  - All New Yorkers are obnoxious.

  - All Southerners are stupid.

Think about what things ignite your judgmental muscle. For me (PH), it's overly opinionated people lacking in facts or perspective. For Michael, it's people trying to control him. Most people have a *hot button* that brings out their judgmental nature. The key is to identify it and become aware of when it comes up then learn how to let it go. Why? Because people do not like judgmental people. Each time you feel your judgmental muscle kicking into gear, ask yourself, "Is this serving me? Does this judgment help or hinder me from achieving my objective?"

We've found there is a rule that can guide you out of a judgmental frame of mind. The rule is: do not go beyond the data! After watching courtroom TV dramas for decades, we recognize the legal phrase *assumes facts not in evidence*. As soon as you recognize that you're doing that simply stop and say, "Hmmm. I'm going to have to think about this."

7. Get Real

No one likes an emotionless robot. We need to know that people are real, capable of feeling, vulnerable and human in order to like them. No one is perfect, and people tend to distrust those who portray themselves as having no faults. People like to pull for the underdog, but they prefer the winner who has overcome some adversity. Be that winner. Tell your story. Show how you fell but grew from it. Give people a reason to get excited about you.

One of our clients is such a person. Several years ago, he was in a serious auto accident that nearly killed him and left him in a coma. He finally emerged, but he had suffered so much damage to his brain that he had to relearn everything. Where many of us would have given up under the weight of such a burden, this man did the opposite. He embraced it and is now writing a book about his many experiences. It's based on getting a second chance to have first experiences. How could you not pull for a guy with such a positive outlook on life?

Spontaneous Vs. Canned and Calculated

Candid, genuine expressions of passion and commitment are worth far more than canned, rehearsed sound bites. Frank Luntz illustrates with this story.

> George W. Bush reached his all-time height of popularity immediately after his impromptu 9-11 speech. It was delivered to rescue workers via a megaphone from the top of a burned-out fire truck buried in the rubble that been the World Trade Center. When one of the workers yelled out, "We can't hear you" Bush responded, "Well I can hear you. The whole world hears you. And the people who knocked down these buildings will hear all of us soon. " Personal, emotional, and spontaneous, he said what every American was thinking and feeling.

> Compare that to John Kerry at the Democratic National Convention when he stepped up to the podium, snapped a salute and said, "I'm John Kerry and I'm reporting for duty." The gesture was obviously planned and calculated and therefore of questionable efficacy.

I (ML) have given several speeches during which I talk about attending military funerals. In every situation, it has been difficult to get through the speech as I stumble on my words and pause to regain my composure. That's just a natural expression of emotion for me. Imagine if I just waltzed through such a speech as though I were talking about the need for a designated rollerblade lane through the central business district. The mismatch would create confusion and probably contempt.

8. Leverage Similarity

Similar on the Outside

Many Native American legends include characters who were said to possess the ability to *shape-shift*. They could change from one physical form to another. Well, that's not what we're asking you to do. Even if it were possible, it's just more change than is called for here. What we're suggesting you do is make it easier for the other person to relate to you. There are some very specific skills or behaviors that will make this possible for you.

To put it into perspective, think of this as the practical application of empathy. Our definition of *practical empathy* is "the things you do to *become* the other person." It's your effort to truly understand that other person. If you wanted to *become* someone else, what would you do? You'd look at him in a new way. You'd notice his facial expressions, the tilt of his head, posture, gestures, and on and on. The point is, the more of those things you notice and adapt to, the more familiar you'll appear to that person. The more familiar you appear, the more he will assume you understand and relate to his life experience.

What are the specific things you should do? Just engage him in conversation, and as he is talking, match his facial expressions and body attitude.

Match the face

People do not know what facial expression they make when they are honestly expressing themselves, but they do recognize when other people are engaged in understanding and relating to them.

Here's what this looks like. Let's say I'm your prospect, and I begin to tell my story. When I get to a point that excites me, I raise my eyebrows. When I get to a point I need to analyze, my eyebrows come together. When I get to a point where I talk about my family or pets, my eyes smile. While I'm doing that, what should you be doing? What most people do is sit and stare, unmoving, like a stuffed animal. If you do not follow me by making the same facial expressions, I will think that you have no idea what I'm talking about, that there is no way on earth that you and I could have any kind of meaningful connection, that you simply do not understand me, and therefore do not value me. Is that what you want?

So, the lesson here is to move your face into the same expressions I make, but do it in a more subtle way. Want to practice?

- Just turn on your TV and watch reality shows. Wherever you can find *real* people, you'll find real facial expressions. Simply match the expressions you see.

- Develop a few archetypes and match their *look*.

    - An exuberant child. This will cause you to raise your eyebrows to show excitement.

    - A scientist. This will cause you to bring your eyebrows together trying to understand complex ideas.

    - A puppy. This will cause you to smile in your eyes.

    - A high achiever. This will cause you to make a *judging* or *calculating* face made by people who seek perfection.

Match the body

The messages sent by body language comprise about half of a person's communication. Thus, if you match what the other person's body is doing, you'll display an understanding that's more important than your understanding of the specific words used. This is a significant area of psychology, and while it is not our purpose to give a class in nonverbal communication or body language here, we do want to give you an understanding of how important this mode of communication is.

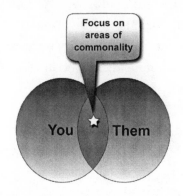

Figure 6-1: Focus on Commonalities

Because you're not in training to be a psychotherapist, you don't need to understand the meanings and motivations behind all the movements and gestures made by the other person. You only need to match the basic angles and attitudes shown to you by the other person. You might think of this as *damage control*, by which you are seeking to keep from breaking rapport with or driving a separation between you and the other person.

Let's look at how people make mistakes with this aspect of connection:

- Imagine that the other person crosses his arms and pulls his head into his shoulders, kind of curling into a ball. Across the desk, you lean back and knit your fingers together behind your head. What kind of connection are you making? None. In fact, you've just broken any connection you might have had.

- Imagine the other person leans forward, getting very close to you over the desk. Across the desk, you turn sideways and look down at the carpet. What kind of connection are you making? None. In fact, you've just broken any connection you might have had.

- Imagine the other person is sitting straight up with his head tilted to the side. Across the desk, you lean in, getting as close as you can. What kind of connection are you making? None. In fact, you've just broken any connection you might have had.

In those scenarios, were you to have simply approximated the same angles and attitudes as the other person, you would have taken a step toward rapport and connection. There is a general formula for building a connection: Match three things about the other person and you've taken a giant step into the connection. Does it work? It certainly does to my (ML) experience.

Many years ago, I (ML) was participating in an experiment to determine if it were possible to connect with a total stranger just through matching the way he or she walked. We were in the largest shopping mall in Houston, Texas and looking at a couple of hundred people walking in a hallway about one hundred yards long. Through the crowd I spotted a person just entering the hall and began walking toward him. I matched the way his feet hit the ground, the angle of his knees, the sway of his hips, the twist of his torso, dip of his shoulders—everything I could see. Then, right as I started to match the angle of his head, I was ten feet from him and looking into the face of a gang member. I thought he would certainly punch me in the nose for mimicking him. Instead, he gave me a head nod. He saw a shared experience in how I was walking. He did not know that I was simply matching his walk.

That was a profound experience, but I duplicated it with the very next person. The lesson became very clear to me: people express their attitudes and life experiences in the way they use their bodies. If you match their bodies, they will see you as familiar, or at least as sharing/understanding some of their experience. I served in the Marine Corps during the sixties. I've spoken with other Marines over the years, and we all swear that we can spot other Marines just by how they walk. They express the Marine Corps experience in their body attitude.

Pam has had the same experience. She wasn't in the military, but through college and corporate life she spent years closely associating with highly analytical people. When we're driving through town, she can spot analytical people just by the way they walk.

The lesson for you is to match the other person in facial expressions and body attitude. This will make it easier for the other person to like you. It will also help you understand that other person's experience. The bigger picture is that when you can inspire someone to like you, he will give you more time to state your case and will give you the benefit of the doubt.

Match the invisible

In teaching people how to read other people, we often get a common question: "I do most of my work over the phone, so how can I read someone over the phone?" It's actually pretty easy to do, but, while we were developing an effective approach to this, we started paying attention to what messages people give over the phone. This was easy to do because, like you, we get calls every day. One of the things we started noticing was a difference in the amount of energy different people put into their communication.

You can hear the difference in how they speak. Some people have a forceful voice and the sound seems to explode out of their mouths. Others have a soft and gentle voice and the sound seems to barely make it from their mouths to the other person's ear.

Obviously, if you are intent on matching the other person, you could do serious harm to your connection by mismatching this energy. Alternately, you can let your own energy adapt to match what you're hearing (or seeing), and that will communicate to the other person that you are similar in that way. Mind you, it usually takes only a slight adjustment to approximate someone's level of energy.

Similar on the Inside

You obviously can't change who you are on the inside—your identity, values, beliefs and interests—simply to connect to another person. What you can do, however, is find the commonalities— the values, beliefs, interests and experiences—that you share with that person.

You can simply ask some questions, then make note of the answers. Those answers will tell you where the commonalities are. Here are some questions you can ask:

- Why did you decide to come here today?

- What are the most important things you want me to do for you?

- What aspect of this (one of the things he or she just listed) is important to you?

- How did that become so important to you?

The answers you get to those questions will paint a picture of that person's values, beliefs, interests and experiences. Here's the important distinction: the information will be important only in the context of that topic. You cannot generalize here.

In your conversation, go backwards through the list to paint your picture of who that person is on the inside. Start with shared interests and experiences then explore beliefs and values. The last thing you would consider addressing is that person's identity. Simply, most people can't explain or describe their identity. They typically tell you what they can do, their capabilities, and you should already know those things. So don't ask, "What's your identity?" because you won't get an answer you can use. Just piece together the various bits of information you hear into a sort of collage representing that person's identity. You'll have everything you need in order to know how to connect with that person.

We've been doing training and coaching in this area for many years and have heard clients say, "I just don't have anything in common with this person." To which we say, "If that's true then perhaps you haven't had the right conversation."

In the 1990s I (PH) worked for Mobil, and my job involved visiting international affiliates to try to get them to use the same processes and systems. At first glance, I didn't seem to have much in common with my African, Indonesian, Japanese or Latin American colleagues. However, after only a little bit of conversation, I found commonalities—something to *connect* us.

I knew that in order to be successful at my job I had to connect with each group, but I looked drastically different from most of the groups I had to connect with. It also seemed as though, as a suit-wearing American from corporate headquarters, I did not have much in common with their values, beliefs, interests or experiences—at least not at first blush.

I learned very quickly that you can always find some connection point if you look hard enough. I'll start with Japan because that was the most difficult one. I found myself sitting across the table from five 50-something Japanese men who each had decided, before I got there, that they were not going to listen to anything I had to say. I had my position in the company, my nationality, ethnicity and gender all working against me. There was little chance that this male-dominated Japanese team was going to find a blonde-haired, blue-eyed corporate representative from Texas in any way credible. I had to shoot for likeable, which meant I had to find something in common with these guys at a values, beliefs, interests or experience level. My connection, as it turned out, came during a smoke break where we shared knowledge of and a passion for...baseball.

In the UK, the similarity was beer and football (soccer) and, to some extent, a shared belief in the value of knowledge and a shared respect for the British intellect. In Jakarta, it was also a shared belief. Specifically, it was a belief in inclusiveness and a sense that the whole is greater than the sum of the parts. I also connected to the Indonesians by truly experiencing their culture and sharing my feelings about those experiences with them.

In Germany, the connection was a shared sense of perfectionism, respect for quality and belief that German engineering is superior to that of the rest of the world. In Beaumont, Texas it was all things cowboy and a healthy respect for the good ole USA; in Singapore, an ability to eat hot peppers; in Paris and Brussels, an appreciation for (and large commitment of time to) eating and drinking.

In all aspects I was just being me. I simply figured out how to emphasize different aspects in different situations for the purpose of making a connection. Bottom line—the more things you share, the more likeable you are.

The Hearing Aid

Most people are visual, meaning that their minds are distracted by things they see, and thus they miss important things others are saying. So we developed a little tool you can use. It's just a simple three-column table we call the *Hearing Aid*. All you have to do is write your notes under the appropriate heading. Here's an abbreviated example:

Connection Points	Content	Values
Fishing	• Uncle Ted took him fishing • Special time together • Loved just being outside	Family Nature/Outdoors Meaningful time //
Camping	• Camp in Yellowstone every summer • Family event • Slow down • Be together as a family	Family // Meaningful time // Slow down Nature/Outdoors
Protecting the environment	• Want others to be able to experience what I did as a kid • Feel compelled to support, protect • Want to set up a fund	Nature/Outdoors Meaningful time // Family Protect/Support

Those notes on the left show where you personally might connect with this person. The ones in the middle are a synopsis of the content, and the notes on the right are that person's values. See the // marks next to a couple of the words? That's how you show the number of times that person repeated those words or expressed those values.

Looking at those notes, you can see that this is a person who loves the outdoors and wants to protect the environment. However, the reason he values the outdoors is because that's how the family can come together and slow down from the hectic pace of modern life. He also values the experience or meaningful time together. With those notes, do you think you could reconnect and engage in a meaningful conversation the next time you meet?

Chapter 7:
What Is Credibility?

All the things we've just covered add up to improved Likeability. Are they important? Absolutely! But typically, Likeability is not enough in a business context. You could be the most likeable person in the world, but still not be able to influence, inspire or close the deal. Other than the possibility that your solution is inappropriate for that client, it's most likely the deal would fall through because that person sees you as likeable but not credible.

Since it's difficult to hit a moving target, let's look at just what Credibility is. The first thing you notice when you attempt to nail this down is that, even at its most tightly defined, Credibility still seems vague. That's because different people refer to it as different things. What we see across the board, however, is that Credibility is a *cluster concept*. It's a combination of other abstract concepts such as (but not limited to) integrity, competence and relevance—all somewhat vague as well. While people openly admit that Credibility is a vital part of their business success, they can't pinpoint what it is. "Michael, I can't describe it, but I know it when I see it."

Our focus is to help make Credibility explicit to you. We want to take Credibility out of the magical, mystical realm and put it on the bottom line so you will not only know what it is, you will also know how to improve the perception of your Credibility in the minds of your target audience.

Looking for Mr. Credibility

As we begin to look closely at your Credibility, what we're actually doing is addressing the *perception* of your Credibility. So what is the *perception* of Credibility? It's the result of your efforts to communicate, demonstrate or prove your actual Credibility. True Credibility is a state of being that you possess. If your Credibility is the message, you need a way to communicate it, but because no two people ever have the same life experiences, no two people receive or interpret a message in the same way. That means the ultimate message gleaned about your Credibility is limited to the perception each person derives from your efforts, after filtering it all through his or her experiences, prejudices and mental wiring.

The hard truth is, no matter how great your personal integrity or competence, it is not you who gets to determine your Credibility. In truth, Credibility can only be given to you by other people. Some people may have had direct experience with you and your Credibility. Others may have only experienced you through media or by reputation. Either way, they have gathered impressions and perceptions that influence how they feel about you.

You have two jobs ahead of you: continue to improve your actual Credibility, and begin to manage the perceptions of your Credibility. That's what this section is all about.

Most Credible Source is a Person Like Me

At first glance, you might think that the most credible spokesperson for a business is the most educated or the most successful professional, such as a doctor, a scientist, or an academic expert. Although in some cases these people may in fact be the most credible, similarity exerts a heavier force.

According to the 2006 *Edelman Trust Study*, a survey of nearly 2000 opinion leaders in eleven countries, the most credible source of information about a company is *a person like me*. Edelman finds that *a person like me* surpasses even doctors and academic experts as a preferred information resource.

We see this play out in advertising campaigns every day. Companies choose regular people to talk about their experiences with the product or service. They purposely choose people who look and sound like the target market. Dove's 2004 *Campaign for Real Beauty* is a classic example. Rather than use supermodels, Dove chose six regular, slightly heavier women to model in bras and panties. The six appeared in television and magazine ads and on billboards across the country. The impact of the ad campaign was huge. Dove's customers responded favorably to the real women ads because they could relate – these were women who looked and sounded like them.

The psychological impact of *a person like* me plays out not only in sales and marketing but also in everyday persuasion. Social psychologist Geoffrey Cohen quantified the impact in a study where he discovered that Democrats were more accepting of a welfare program if they believed it was proposed by a fellow Democrat, even when the proposal came from a Republican and was quite restrictive. Predictably, Cohen found the same effect for Republicans who were far more likely to approve a generous welfare program if they though it was proposed by a fellow Republican.

Familiarity and Variability Enhance Credibility

In the previous section, we discussed familiarity as an aspect of Likeability. Familiarity is also a component of Credibility. The more familiar that people are with you and your message, the more likely they are to perceive both as credible.

Studies into Credibility and influence suggest that multiple exposures to a statement validate the statement in a receiver's mind. There are two explanations that account for this *truth effect*. They're called *subjective familiarity* and *source variability*. We know from research by Anne Roggeveen that the more we hear something, the more likely we are to believe it is true.

Recall the slogans you've seen and heard. Were you ever influenced by a slogan to buy a product? Repeating simple messages is the psychology behind commoditized products. Can you name the advertisers for each of the following? Why do you think you remember them?

- _____ brings good things to life

- Like a good neighbor _____ is there

- Reach out and touch someone _____

- Have it your way _____

- When it absolutely, positively has to be there overnight

  _____

- Let your fingers do the walking _____

- You asked for it, you got it _____

Research also suggests how you can use this information:

- The more variable the sources (different people or sources that say it) the more likely we are to believe it is true.

- If we hear a message from the same source at different times, we are likely to subconsciously believe it came from different sources and therefore are more likely to believe it is true.

Here is how this plays out in your world. You read about a company in *Barrons*, then you hear a similar report on CNBC. When your financial advisor mentions the same company, sharing a similar opinion, you attribute Credibility to both the message and the messenger. This brings validity to the thought that people are known by the quality of the information they share.

Marketers and advertisers have learned to capitalize on the psychology of familiarity. In the early 1990s, we taught many professionals how to implement a sequential approach to marketing known as wave marketing or drip marketing. That approach is based on building familiarity. A second way to build on this idea is to employ multiple media sources to deliver the same message. And still a third way to use this psychology is with testimonials. According to Roggeveen, the ultimate in truth-effect advertising is the repetition of statements with different credible endorsers associated with each repetition.

Of course, the key phrase there is *credible endorsers* because as you've already seen, it's the Credibility of the person endorsing a person, product, service or idea that will tip the scales of our decision making mechanism. For example, when Michael Lovas endorses Trek bicycles no one pays attention, but when Lance Armstrong endorses Trek, the entire cycling world pays attention. Put another way, you can have the perfectly phrased argument, but if you (the person delivering it) are not perceived as credible your message will have limited impact.

Credibility of the Messenger Determines Message Impact

In a paper published in the *International Journal of Communication* in January of 2007, Ned Rinalducci made the following observations:

- The greater a source's perceived expertise and trustworthiness, the greater the ability to produce an attitude change.

- Highly trustworthy and expert spokespersons induce a greater positive attitude toward the position they advocate than do communicators with less Credibility.

- Traditionally (as far back as Aristotle), the construct of source Credibility has been thought to involve a source's knowledge of the subject that he or she discusses, as well as his or her veracity, and his or her attitude toward the well-being of the receiver.

In plain language what that means is: In order for your message to have impact and influence, you must be perceived as credible. Credibility comes from more than what you know; it also comes from who you are and who others see you as. The Credibility of you and your message is directly affected by the perceived Credibility of the source of the testimonial or endorsement.

Assumptions About Credibility Are Not Always Logical

The focus of this chapter is how we determine Credibility. Sadly, that determination is not always logical or based on fact. As humans we possess many assumptions—beliefs, attitudes, ideas and other preconceived notions. We either possess assumptions about, or from, them regarding literally everything we can name. The point is, we often make assumptions about Credibility based on implication.

A classic example of these types of assumptions comes from the Orson Welles radio adaptation of the H. G. Wells novel *The War of the Worlds*. The program began with a news bulletins used to build (or imply) Credibility. The assumption was that if it's news, it has to be credible. It also built Credibility by interviewing seemingly credible people about the invasion. They were fictitious but seemed so real. A few of them were: Professor Farrell of the Mount Jennings Observatory, Professor Morse of McMillan University, and General Montgomery Smith (Commander of the Trenton State Militia). The public believed the invasion was real primarily because of the perceived Credibility of the medium carrying the message (news) and the people talking about it.

In Carl Hovland's studies of persuasion, we find more evidence that the persuasiveness of the message is directly related to the perceived Credibility of the messenger. In a 1953 experiment by Hovland, subjects were played a message that recommended more lenient treatment of juvenile offenders. One group was told the source of the message was a judge in a juvenile court. The other group was told the source was an alleged drug dealer.

It's not surprising that when the subjects were assessed immediately after hearing the messages, they found the high-Credibility source (the judge) to be more persuasive. Three weeks later they were again assessed. This time, only half the subjects were reminded who the source was. It turned out that where there was a reminder, the subjects maintained their original position, but where there was none the researchers found a significant decrease in the persuasion of the high-Credibility condition.

Suggestibility is determined by Credibility. In a similar study, researchers Sorokin and Baldyreff played listeners two recordings of a classical music piece, each bearing exactly the same performance. Listeners were told in advance that one of the performances had been judged as significantly better by music critics. Ninety-six percent of subjects considered the performances to be different and fifty-nine percent agreed with the alleged opinion of the experts.

The point of this discussion is simply to demonstrate that people make judgments about Credibility that aren't always reasonable or based on logic. The lesson we want you to gain here is that the better you understand what influences perceptions of Credibility, the better you can be at demonstrating your own Credibility.

Now let's dig deeper into how people make those initial determinations of Credibility.

How Do People Decide if You Are Credible?

In this section we're going to cover two topics: implied or assumed Credibility based on title, profession, association or public persona; and first impressions—the immediate judgments people make about your Credibility when they first meet you.

Assumed Credibility

Earlier, we went into detail to explain how first impressions affect Likeability. You learned that the majority of the first impression you give to someone else takes place in that person's subconscious. You also learned some of the specific things you can do to improve your chances of making a positive first impression.

Now we're going to take you one step backwards in time from that first impression. We're going to look at what takes place prior to that first impression. We're going to look at *assumed Credibility*. This is the Credibility (or lack of Credibility) assigned to you based on preconceived notions of what you do and for whom you do it. It looks like this (Figure 7-1):

Figure 7-1: Levels of Credibility

The small center circle is where we find you and your personal Credibility. The outlying circles are where we find your *assumed Credibility*. Starting from this inside circle, let's assume John Smith actually is a credible professional who is highly respected by his clients and his community.

As we move to the next circle, he takes on a certain amount of Credibility simply by being a financial advisor. People have certain preconceived notions about the Credibility of financial advisors, and John Smith inherits those perceptions and impressions. Good or bad, they come with the territory.

Moving to the outer-most circle, John Smith also inherits Credibility based on where and with whom he works. In this case, preconceived notions and impressions of Merrill Lynch will be automatically assigned to John Smith.

As professions, companies and industries float into and out of favor, John Smith will experience the increase in his related Credibility, and also the related loss of Credibility. For example, if being a financial advisor or association with Merrill Lynch is reported negatively in the media, he could take a Credibility hit in the eyes of his target market(s).

What Professions or Associations Are the Most Credible?

Let's use John Smith and the three circles as a model as we look at different situations and contexts. Think of professions that are considered more credible. What are they? What if John Smith were a Supreme Court Judge? Would he have greater Credibility? What if he were a used car salesman? Maybe not so much Credibility then.

The Public Relations Society of America (PRSA) asked thousands of Americans the question, "What professions are the most credible?" The answers were tabulated and put into a list of professions arranged in order. It's called the "Credibility Index." (Details are included in the Appendix.) We cite it here for two reasons: 1) Simply to illustrate that certain professions are generally seen as more (or less) credible than others. 2) To give you the experience of determining for yourself who is more credible.

Here are some of the professions from the Credibility Index, plus one called "Your own profession." Your assignment is to put them into order of most credible to least credible. (See *Credibility Index* in the Appendix for the real rankings.)

- Teacher
- School official
- High-ranking military officer
- Member of the armed forces
- Supreme Court justice
- National expert
- Local business owner
- Ordinary citizen

- Local religious leader

- Your own profession

The PRSA list is similar to one developed by New Zealand's *National Business Review*. They found the following:

Most hated professions	Most respected professions
1. Politician	1. Doctor
2. Lawyer	2. Nurse
3. Real Estate agent	3. Teacher
4. MP (member of parliament)	4. Firefighter
5. Journalist	5. Ambulance driver
6. Advertising executive	6. Soldier
7. Car dealer	7. Scientist
8. Company director	8. Police officer
9. Accountant	9. Caregiver

First Impressions of Credibility

When people first meet you, what sort of data are their minds collecting about you, and how does this input affect your Credibility? In addition to the assumptions they make about who you are, what you do and for whom you do it, they are also gathering information from the following sources:

- *Your facial expressions.* Even strangers can recognize the disconnect between words and facial expressions. Looking unsure or frightened while making strong claims causes people to discount your Credibility.

- *Your body.* We make assumptions about body type. Fat is seen as lazy and less competent, where lean and fit is seen as smart and successful. Whatever your body type make it work for you.

- *Your movements and gestures.* Bold gestures are interpreted as confident. Gestures close to the body are interpreted as timid.

- *How (or if) you touch them.* Ever go to shake someone's hand but that person goes to hug you? Ever release your grip while shaking hands but the other person hangs on? Human skin is both sensitive and interpretive. How you touch other people gives them a lot of information about you. What does your touch say?

- *The distance you keep from them.* Like touch, distance is personal. It's also cultural. The safest approach is to assume the other person does not want you within a three feet radius.

- *Your clothes.* Credible dress is professional, *put together* and smart. Credible is classic style, not ultra modern or flashy.

- *Your presentation materials.* We attended a program by a world-renowned researcher. His slides were boring and amateurish. Not only did we notice, but the entire audience was talking about the slides and not the content of the program. Your slides represent the quality you want to impart.

- *The sound of your voice.* Tune your radio to a news station. What kind of voices do you hear? They're deep and resonant—that's credible. If your voice is high and/or thin, you have some work to do. It is possible to completely change the sound of your voice.

- *Your energy level.* High energy is interpreted as interested and proactive. Low energy is interpreted as lackadaisical or disinterested.

- *Your relation to time.* In business, time is not determined by you. It's determined by your prospect or client. If you are late to a meeting, it tells them that you do not value their time. Credible people budget their time like money, but they also are open to investing as much time as necessary to fulfill promises.

- *How you smell.* Business meetings are different from romantic interludes. While cologne and perfumes are acceptable in one, they are offensive in the other.

- *Your office.* The location, furnishings, size and configuration of your office tell people what you value. Picture your office from their perspective. What does it say?

- *Paralanguage (grunts).* Emitting an uh-huh or hmmmm at the right time demonstrates to the other person that you are right there following what he or she says. Your Credibility strategy is to form as close a connection as possible. If the other person thinks you're not following him or her, you lose the connection.

Every aspect of the things in this list is important. It all adds up to who you are as a source of multiple messages, like a hologram. We tell our clients, "Everything you say, write or do says something about your Credibility. The better you understand and manage those messages, the more effective you can become at being perceived as the credible professional you actually are. However, if you ignore this advice and neglect to take control of the messages, you will likely become a casualty of your decision."

Intention

It is impossible to perfectly manage every message you transmit. That's because there are simply too many variations of verbal and nonverbal messages being transmitted by you at any given time.

A simple vocal inflection or facial expression could contaminate the entire meaning of what you're saying. The best you can do is understand the many ways people get information from you, then trust in the truth and congruence of your intention. If your intention is honorable, most of your messages will show that. If your intention is self-serving, your messages will conflict.

Nonverbals Tell the Story

If integrity, competence and congruence are fundamental to actual Credibility, then perception is fundamental to communicating your Credibility to your target market(s). Again, the point here is to learn how to be more effective when you communicate, demonstrate or prove your actual Credibility. The perception each person derives from your efforts represents the value your efforts have for that person. Your Credibility is entirely in the minds of your target market(s).

Congruence

Earlier in this book, you learned that Likeability is determined by the congruence of verbal and nonverbal messages when you're expressing feelings and emotions. In terms of Credibility, the most important nonverbal quality is the congruence between your verbal and nonverbal expressions when you're presenting relevant/factual information. In other words, do you have the character to walk the talk or just talk some more? Are you consistent in your words and actions, or are you giving conflicting messages?

This congruence includes an extremely wide variety of elements. The more effective you are at coordinating and aiming them, the greater Credibility you can develop. Refer back to our earlier list of elements and consider what it looks and sounds like to be congruent across all of them.

Imagine that you are interviewing a job candidate who is describing how he closed a major deal worth millions of dollars. But his stammers show you someone who is insecure telling what is supposedly his own story. This incongruence detracts from his Credibility.

Imagine a person is interviewing for a job as a banker. His resume shows exactly the right experience, and he seems competent enough, but he simply looks more like a surfer than a banker. We have expectations of how a banker should look (conservative, clean cut, etc.), and this candidate, though qualified, gives us an incongruent picture. Chances are we will not be able to justify or get past the incongruence.

The Look of Credibility

Over the years that we've been studying Credibility, one of the areas that has most fascinated us is the *look* of Credibility. While there is some room for variety here, we've identified a certain credible look that we see more often than any other. Someone with this look could merely stand silently and still be perceived as credible. To understand this look, let's first go in the opposite direction and explore what is not a credible look. Our favorite source for this information is Virginia Satir, psychotherapist and author.

Satir identified four behavior patterns that people fall into when they're dealing with stress. Realize that stress can be generated when a prospect gives you an objection. Realize, as well, that none of these archetypes is credible; so if you recognize yourself, seek to make some adjustments. Satir's four behavior patterns are:

The Blamer. This person responds by attempting to overpower. He is loud, tyrannical and looking for someone or something to blame. If the Blamer makes his pitch and is hit with an objection, he will attack the prospect: "It's firms like *yours* that make these costs so high." Other common terms for a Blamer are Bully, Dictator, and Hanging Judge.

The Distractor. The Distractor does whatever it takes to divert focus onto someone or something else. She is a moving target, in constant motion. If the Distractor delivers a presentation that is met with an objection, she will do what we call the *tap dance.* That means she will divert the responsibility to something or someone else. Think of the Distractor as the Simulated Woman, diverting attention to keep people from discovering her insecurity or lack of substance.

The Placator. The Placator caves in, both physically and emotionally, to the dominant person. He cannot stand up for himself, nor can he disagree. It is unlikely that a Placator would make a presentation, preferring to remain behind the scenes; but, if the Placator is met with resistance he will apologize and back up quickly enough for you to see that he is unencumbered by a spine. Some other common names for a Placator are Doormat and Victim.

The Computer. Attempting to lose herself inside verbiage is how the Computer covers her feelings. She is unemotional, inexpressive, and verbose. If a long sentence is appropriate, she will add even more onto it. A Computer would likely not be delivering a presentation, but if she did and was met with an objection, she would inundate the prospect with confusing data. We've heard people refer to Computers by saying, "The lights are on, but there's nobody home."

Meet the Commander

The opposite of the Satir behavior styles is what we call the commander. Let's look at the various qualities of the commander:

- **Eye contact**—direct without staring. Not afraid to look you in the eye. Focused, not roaming the room.

- **Dress**—one step above the rest of the people. You will likely never find this person wearing *business casual*. There is a touch of formality here.

- **Posture**—symmetrical, balanced, firm, rooted. Arms symmetrical or in a neutral position at his or her side.

- **Gestures**—firm and definitive. Very little bending at the wrist.

- **Face**—serious, reserved and attentive. His or her face shows that he or she is giving you every bit of his or her attention.

- **Space**—respectful of your personal space, but not timid about being close.

- **Time**—right now. No wasted seconds. You recognize that his or her time is important and he or she is sharing it with you, so your time is important to him or her.

- **Voice**—in charge, under control, firm. Speaks in short bursts of relevant content. Stays on point.

- **Listening**—emotive. Takes the time and makes the effort to understand the factual content, as well as the emotional content.

The Political Posture

As we write this chapter, it is still primary season leading up to the 2008 presidential election. We've seen a throng of candidates come and go. They have all had something in common—they know how to *look* credible. They've most likely worked with a speech coach to perfect how they deliver their points but if you know what they're not doing or saying, you can see the cracks or *negative space* in their persona.

What's wrong? Where do they falter? Where do they lose their Credibility? We believe it comes down to one quality that eventually gets stripped away. It's the congruence between their intention and their message. Over time and many debates, we get to see them looking good and going through their *act* in a polished manner. But their acts do not fit all situations, and when there is a question or situation that falls outside of their rehearsed responses that's when we get to see the *real* person. That is when we get to see their inconsistencies.

The lesson to learn from the political arena is to pay attention to how they look. Pay attention to how they stand and gesture, and leave it at that. Let those things *accessorize* how the real you communicates. In the end, while few people look credible in their underwear, that's when your real Credibility will shine. Can you be as credible under the spotlight as you can when no one is looking? Just be sure to put that real Credibility into an attractive package.

Can Looks Predict a Successful CEO?

In pursuing the truth about the look of Credibility, we came across another eye-opening study. According to a study by Tufts University psychologists Nicholas Rule and Nalini Ambady, the answer to the question (Can looks predict a successful CEO?) is yes.

The researchers showed one hundred college students black-and-white headshots of fifty Fortune 1000 CEOs—a fairly homogeneous-looking group, made up almost entirely of middle-aged white men. The researchers asked the students to rate the executives on: personality traits (such as competence and trustworthiness), and how well they thought the person would lead a company.

The results: The results were based entirely on what the students saw in the photos. CEOs who scored high on measures of power (competence, dominance and facial maturity) were in many cases the ones who ran companies with the biggest overall profits. On the other hand, the ones who were rated high on measures of warmth (such as Likeability and trustworthiness) didn't necessarily match up with successful companies.

The results suggest that Credibility is more associated with success at this level than Likeability. The study also suggests that success has a certain *look* of competence, power and facial maturity. Nalini Ambady, a Tufts professor and one of the study's authors, said, "What's not clear is whether people pick CEOs because they look a certain way, or if people look a certain way once they become CEOs."

The study didn't ask participants why they thought one CEO looked more competent or trustworthy than another. The judgments being measured were spontaneous, gut-level responses. This lends support to a growing argument among psychologists who study decision-making that when people come to quick conclusions without much information their decisions are often good ones. The study's authors point out, "These findings suggest that naïve judgments may provide more accurate assessments of individuals than well-informed judgments can." In other words, the perceptions you give to other people are often devoid of logic, but in many situations those perceptions are all you have to work with.

The Face of Credibility

We have discovered that the world generally perceives two faces. One is friendly and likeable; it's the face of someone you might confide in. The other is serious and attentive. This is the face you trust to act on your behalf. We're often asked to justify the difference between the two faces. It's simply the right tool for the right job. Sometimes you want to be friendly and sometimes you want to be credible. It all depends on your purpose at that moment.

What makes a face look credible? We've learned that a credible face is serious, attentive and confident. What else influences the perception of Credibility? According to Brandeis University's Leslie Zebrowitz, author of *Reading Faces: Window to the Soul*, someone with a more mature face is likely to be judged as more credible than someone with a baby face (described as round face, large eyes, small nose and small chin) even when the two are seen to be of equal age, sex and attractiveness. Those with baby face features are perceived as more childlike and consequently less competent. People with more mature faces are judged to be more dominant, physically stronger and intellectually shrewd.

Zebrowitz references a study where images of U.S. presidents Reagan and Kennedy were morphed to increase the baby-faced characteristics. The result? Their perceived dominance, strength and cunning decreased significantly.

In 2004, research by Keating and colleagues (referenced in "Do Babyfaced Adults Receive More Help?") illustrated that adding baby-face features to photos changed viewers' perceptions. Digitized images of African-American and European-American adult male and female faces were made to look babyish by substituting enlarged eyes and lips for normal ones. In other photos, eyes and lips were reduced in size to make faces look mature. As expected, the baby-like features made adults appear submissive, weak, naive, compassionate, and honest.

Are babyfaced people actually less competent?

Research suggests that our initial assumptions about people with a baby face are that they are less competent and lacking in physical strength, social dominance and intellectual shrewdness. We often conclude that baby-faced adults are naive, submissive and weak.

But is this actually true? Does perception equal reality? Zebrowitz suggests that in reality the opposite is true. "Baby-faced people are more intelligent, better educated and more assertive" than their mature-looking counterparts. She suggests that this may be because they overcompensate for society's expectations. Once again, the perception trumps reality.

Can you *see* competence?

Princeton's Alex Todorov conducted research in 2004 to determine the importance of political candidates' facial appearance in election success. More than 800 people were shown pairs of photographs. Each pair contained similar-looking candidates who had competed against each other in elections for the U.S. Senate or House of Representatives.

After seeing each face for less than a second, the participants were asked to judge them according to various criteria including intelligence, Likeability, age, competence, trustworthiness, charisma, attractiveness and familiarity. If a participant recognized any of the candidates' faces, the judgment for that pair was discounted.

The researchers found a strong correlation between those candidates judged "competent" and election wins. Judging on this *look* of competence alone, participants correctly predicted the winners in about 70 percent of the congressional races.

Marketing professor J. Scott Armstrong of the University of Pennsylvania's Wharton School conducted a similar study using the 2008 U.S. presidential candidates. To find people who wouldn't recognize the candidates, he enlisted students in South Australia and New Zealand. Using twenty-four real and potential candidates, participants were asked to rate each candidate's competence on a scale of one to ten.

Hillary Clinton ranked the highest, followed by General Wesley Clark and Senator Barack Obama. Senator John McCain led the Republicans but still trailed the top six Democrats. The least competent-looking of the twenty-four were Governor Bill Richardson of New Mexico, former governor of Arkansas Mike Huckabee, and former Senator Fred Thompson. Figure 7-2 includes photos of the top three and the bottom three. This is a grouping we put together using publicly available photos. These are not the ones used by Armstrong in the study. The purpose is simply to provide you with a quick reminder of who we're talking about. Are there any immediate impressions that come to mind when you compare the top row faces against the bottom row?

Figure 7-2 - Armstrong Study Results -
Most Competent and Least Competent Faces

Although both the Todorov and Armstrong studies focused on scoring competence in a face and then looking to see if there was a correlation between that determination and election results, we suggest that the judgments were actually about more than just competence. What do you think participants were actually judging? Although Zebrowtiz's baby face versus mature face conclusions explain, in part, the perceptions, our sense is that there is something more. Could it be that we humans are inherently good at picking a winner and what we are actually registering is Credibility and Likeability?

The Look that Works in Politics

When we were writing our book *Face Values*, we gave ourselves a challenge. What could you tell about someone just by looking at his or her face? For example, could you look at people in a crowd and tell who was more competent and who was more likeable? Pam and I can do that with pretty good accuracy, but we're not alone.

Washington University Marketing Professor Michael Lewis and co-author JoAndrea Hoegg from the University of British Columbia examined 112 congressional elections in 2000 and 2002. Lewis and Hoegg found that the look of the individual candidates seemed to transfer information about their personal characteristics. "Republicans tend to do better when they look like a high-school quarterback or a CEO—square jaw, cropped hair," Lewis said. "Democrats did better when they had the look of a college professor."

In the research, participants looked at pictures showing pairs of opposing candidates in the congressional elections. The participants were asked to indicate which candidate appeared more competent, more intelligent, more likable and more trustworthy. The researchers chose congressional, rather than presidential, elections because most congressional candidates aren't well known. Thus, participants would not come into the study **with** preconceived notions of each candidate.

The researchers found that candidates who **were** labeled as more competent and more trustworthy were more often identified as Republican, while those who were labeled as more likeable or intelligent were often identified as Democrats. One amusing implication we see from this is that people assume a disconnect between competence and intelligence.

The Face of a President

A great way to get a sense of what Americans vote for in a face can be found in a fabulous video by Gordon Scott (available on YouTube at http://www.youtube.com/watch?v=xWTWBO8DY8g). Watch each president morph into his successor from George Washington to George W. Bush.

Until I (PH) watched this video, I wasn't aware of the commonalities among facial structure. The more common facial structure for a President is the more angular, mature-looking face. Interestingly, this pattern began to change a bit with Truman, Eisenhower, and Kennedy having a much rounder and more baby-face-like structure. The same is true of Gerald Ford, Bill Clinton and George W. Bush.

The Value of Looking the Part

We talked earlier about assumptions—we expect a professional to look a certain way. I (PH) have a dear friend who is a Mary Kay representative. Although I'm not a big fan of the cosmetics, I am impressed by the commitment of the MK representatives to *look the part*. By *look the part* I mean they recognize that their Credibility is tied to their *look*—their makeup and dress. After all, that's what they're selling. Here's how one representative described it:

"So many people in Mary Kay get upset when they have to dress up a little. I'll admit, I sometimes gripe about it myself; but it is so important to understand how image affects credibility! We work in the cosmetics business—of course we have to look the part! This is why the company originally wanted consultants to wear pantyhose. It was not to make us miserable. It was to make us credible."

Authority and the Power of a Uniform

In Dallas, Texas the Mary Kay reps are recognizable throughout the city. They appear to wear a uniform—in addition to driving pink cars. Also in Dallas is EDS, the company started by Ross Perot. EDS had a strict dress code. In a conversation with representatives of EDS in the early nineties, I was told that when a new employee did not wear the right suit to fit the company's image the company would buy the right suit and have it delivered to that person. Of course, the cost would be deducted from his or her pay.

We all see many different kinds of uniforms during a typical day, but not all of them represent credibility. You walk into a restaurant and see the workers in their orange uniforms. Do you assume they have any credibility? Doubtful. You see a group of workers on the side of the highway. They're inmates from the county jail and are wearing uniforms. Do you assume they have any credibility? You come to an intersection and a police officer puts up his hand to stop you. Do you assume he has any credibility? Probably. What's the difference?

Police use uniforms to send a message. That message might be, "We're bigger, stronger and better armed than you." I (ML) spent three years in the Marine Corps and watched how people responded to us in our uniforms. If you've ever seen a platoon of Marines marching, you know immediately there is power in their uniforms.

What's really going on here? Structure and control. Some people are put into uniforms to convey the message that they are there to serve you—they give you the structure to be in control. Others are put into uniforms to convey the message that they are there to take control. The next time you stand in your closet and ponder what to wear, think about where your wardrobe will place you on the Credibility continuum. On one end are the fast food servers. On the other end are the Marines. If you want people to pay attention to you, move toward the Marines. Assemble your wardrobe like a uniform, and treat it with great respect (flag pin optional).

Research by Leonard Bickman illustrates the power of a uniform. In one of Bickman's experiments he had a man stop pedestrians and ask them to either pick up paper bags, move from where they were standing or give money to a perfect stranger. It worked like this: The man would stop the pedestrian, point to another person nearly fifty feet away and tell the pedestrian that the other man had over parked and didn't have any change to pay the meter. He would then tell the pedestrian to go give the man the necessary change. Hidden researchers watched to see how many people complied when the experimenter was dressed in normal street clothes versus when he was dressed as a security guard.

After giving the command, the man would go around a corner so he was out of the pedestrian's sight. Incredibly, almost all of the pedestrians obeyed when he was dressed in uniform, even after he was gone! But when he was dressed in street clothes, less than half of the pedestrians complied with his request. The uniform made the difference.

In another study, researchers Lawrence and Watson found that individuals asking for contributions to law enforcement and healthcare campaigns gathered more donations when wearing sheriffs' and nurses' uniforms than when they just dressed normally.

The Sound of Credibility

As important as the look of Credibility is, it is actually secondary to the sound of Credibility. If you don't like the sound of your delivery, chances are neither does anyone else. That's just the start of the bad news.

We know from the research that the way we talk (speed, pauses, pronunciation, volume, etc.) triggers certain judgments about our Credibility. People seem to have an innate *competence detector* as well as the previously discussed *trust detector*. Research by Brandeis University Professor Leslie Zebrowitz suggests that "strangers can judge intelligence at levels significantly better than chance from brief exposures to a target's face, voice and other nonverbal cues."

Work by University of Victoria researchers Reynolds and Gifford suggests that auditory cues are more strongly related to intelligence than visual ones. Reynolds and Gifford found that the following speaking styles are interpreted as higher intelligence:

- Less halting speech

- More standard use of language

- Speaking more words

- Speaking each word clearly

- Speaking faster

What does this mean? If you are excellent at thinking quickly on your feet, then you are likely not much affected by it. However, if you're like most of us, when you have to think on your feet your mouth has to wait for your brain to catch up and give directions. Thus, your delivery is peppered with halting stutters and stammers. Listeners perceive such a delivery as evidence that you lack a certain amount of mental snap. Today, the best-known example of this pattern is George W. Bush. You can always tell when he has gotten away from his talking points. He tends to stammer and the rate of speech slows down.

How can you use it? Prepare. Our own observations have shown us overwhelmingly that when a person is prepared, he can improvise all day long and deliver powerful answers in a convincing style. If you were going to participate in a formal debate on a certain subject, wouldn't you prepare? If you were going to be interviewed for a new job, wouldn't you prepare? If you were going to interviewed on TV, wouldn't you prepare? Every time you speak on something important to you, you need to be prepared. The less prepared you are, the more halting your speech will be. That's just what happens when people try to speak while they attempt to formulate their answers.

For five years, I (ML) hosted an online radio interview show. I would interview thought leaders and executives in the financial industry. During our *getting to know you* conversation, the guests were always charming and intelligent. As soon as I announced that we were recording, many of them turned into stammering idiots. Even in our own preparation to lead seminars, Pam and I will alert each other when we've fallen into that stammering idiot pattern. We stop, back up and start over.

Regional Dialects

Pam and I debated whether or not to include this topic in our book. On one hand, regional dialects can cause a strongly negative interpretation. On the other hand, it's not all that easy to do anything about it.

Pam hails from South Carolina and my roots are in New Orleans. Both of us are children of the Deep South and grew up speaking different, but distinctive, regional dialects. The first time I ever heard my own voice was on a recording of a presentation I made in tenth grade speech class. I thought someone had pulled a practical joke on me. I was mortified that I sounded so ignorant.

Being from the American South, both of us are sensitive to how other people talk. Specifically, we are sensitive to whether or not the dialects we hear imply Credibility or something less. Being from the South, we understand full well that prejudice is quick to stick to someone who elongates his vowels and drops an occasional R.

In an article by Cody Lyon on southern accents, Patricia Cukor-Avila, an associate professor of English and linguistics at the University of North Texas said that people outside the South often associate the Southern accent with laziness, ignorance and backward thinking. All of these associations have been perpetuated by years of movies, television and other media. The result for Southerners is a reaction that Cukor-Avila calls *linguistic insecurity*.

Lest we think that it's just a figment of regional imagination, there is a telling study conducted in the heart of the North that validates this prejudice. It's a 1999 study by Michigan State University professor Dennis Preston. He asked 150 southeastern Michigan residents to rank the *correctness* of English spoken in all fifty states. The South as a whole ranked the lowest, with Alabama at the bottom of the list. The bottom line is this: when we talk about perception, the way you sound when you talk has a great deal to do with that perception.

Professor Preston says, "There are two things going on in America: You either went to school and learned how to talk good, which is what Northerners think about themselves, or you didn't, which has been a common image people in the North have of the South."

Fact is, dialects are simply bits of nonverbal data. You add them into the mix. If they work for you, then you're in luck. If they don't work for you, then you have a lot of difficult and tedious work ahead of you to retrain your tongue and lips to form new sounds over your life-long vocabulary. Breaking speech habits is really hard. We know because both Pam and I have done it.

Speed

There is evidence that a slower speed of delivery increases the retention of the information; however, there's more here than meets the ear.

With that thought in mind, you might think that communicators should decrease speed in order to be credible especially if dealing with a complex topic. The research shows exactly the opposite—that an increase in speed is likely to be more persuasive and credible. This probably connects with the notion that speed of delivery equates to the perception of competence.

The assumption is that if you can speak fast about a complex issue, then you must have a powerful grasp of what you're talking about. It's not necessarily as simple as that. Again, we bump into implied Credibility and preconceived notions. For example, in the South, where people tend to talk slower, it is commonly thought that people who speak faster aren't trustworthy.

Speaking fast can be helpful if you are at risk of being interrupted by someone with an opposing perspective. It can also help you if your arguments are weak, as it doesn't give your audience time to process your arguments. However, if what you have to say is strong, it can be useful to slow down precisely in order to allow cognitive processing to take place. We teach our clients to vary the speed of their delivery, otherwise they start to sound like a metronome.

The Language of Credibility

Accuracy. Research shows that the more accurate your language and your content, the more credible you are perceived. In a paper published by the *Newspaper Research Journal* in January 2002, the author stressed the link between accuracy and Credibility. "Accuracy is the foundation of media credibility. If journalists cannot get their facts straight, how can readers trust the media to convey and interpret the news reliably? According to a national survey commissioned by the American Society of Newspaper Editors (ASNE), even small errors feed public skepticism about a newspaper's Credibility."

Words. The actual words you use also make a difference in the perception of your Credibility. If your information is complex or technical, you are better served to reference facts and talk about *factual or accurate* data, rather than referring to *honest, truthful, or credible* data. The reason is logical: accurate data is more important and tends to be more credible because it is a statement of fact rather than someone's explanation or opinion.

Choose facts over opinion. For example, you wouldn't say, "I think…" Rather, you'd say, "The facts suggest…" Similarly, words like *attested to* are far less effective than *certified* because the former is perceived to be about human judgment and the latter suggests a specific process or procedure followed, along with a guarantee.

The Character of Credibility

Our primary focus thus far in this chapter has been judgments and assumptions people make about your credibility when they first meet you. As much as we hate to admit it, it is possible to appear to be credible without actually being credible. But here's the kicker—without actually being credible, you will not be able to sustain the perception of credibility over time.

In order to maintain credibility, you must demonstrate the personal and behavioral characteristics of Credibility. These characteristics include:

- Integrity (a combination of honesty, congruence, accountability and humility)

- Competence

- Relevance

- Objectivity

- Results

Let's look at each of them so you'll have a clear understanding of how they can work for you.

1. Integrity

Integrity is a combination of honesty, congruence, accountability and humility.

Honesty

To be credible you must be overwhelmingly honest—so honest that people never question whether or not what you say is the truth. Kouzes and Posner in *Credibility* note that, "Of all the attributes of Credibility, there is one that is unquestionably of greatest importance: Honesty. The dimension of honesty accounts for more of the variance in believability than all of the other factors combined."

A 2003 survey by organizational-consulting firm Right Management Consultants (as noted in *The Transparency Edge*) asked 570 full-time, white-collar employees, "What is the most important trait or attribute that the leader of your company should possess?" The top trait was honesty, with 24 percent of respondents naming it as the most important trait in a leader. The other top four were: integrity/morals/ethics (16 percent); caring or compassion (7 percent); fairness (6.5 percent); and good relationships with employees, including approachability and listening skills (6 percent).

As you would likely expect, honesty and trustworthiness are key components of Credibility. The people sitting across the table from you will ask themselves questions such as: Is this person honest? Can I believe what he or she is telling me? Does he or she have my best interest in mind or his or her own?

Transparency is an important aspect of honesty. People don't trust what they can't see. A surefire way to damage trust and ultimately credibility is to hide, or be less than transparent about, the important details of your business. This may include information about costs, process, relationships or interests. Ultimately, transparency means being open and honest about your agenda, your intent, and the *what's in it for you* aspect of business.

Congruence

When we experience other people, we are actually experiencing the entire person, and a part of our mind is looking for inconsistencies. In other words, we have a natural BS Detector that is filtering for people who say one thing but may mean something different. When other people experience us, they are looking for a kind of teamwork accountability, but the team is the inner and outer us. It requires us to be consistent or congruent in actions and words.

Psychotherapist and author Virginia Satir said about congruence that every time you talk, all of you talks. Whenever you utter words, your face, voice, body, breathing, and muscles are talking too. As strange as it sounds, we've noticed that in about half the population, their hairline talks! Congruence is when all those things say the same thing. When they're not in harmony, there is no congruence. That's a polite way of saying that our BS Detector went off and alerted us that someone could be lying.

Corporate Congruence

We see this in people, of course, but we also see it in corporations. In fact, we did a little experiment on this topic a few years ago. We were looking to see if corporations were sending mixed messages, so we went to different corporate websites and picked out the values words imbedded in the text. Then we matched those words with their corporate behaviors. The most glaring discrepancy was committed by a global oil corporation that claimed proudly that their people were their most important asset. Unfortunately, their website showed no photos of people and their record of how they treated their employees was dismal. That's called *incongruence*. People see it. They hear it. They feel it. It causes them to stop liking you, to withhold any credibility and, when possible, to stop buying from you.

Accountability

Another element of Credibility that comes across in language is *Accountability*. In credible language, your words show that you not only take responsibility but can also be held accountable. See the subtle difference between, "I am *responsible* for protecting my client's assets," versus, "I am *accountable* for protecting my client's assets." Accountability trumps responsibility because it implies enforcement and perhaps even punishment for failure.

Do you know people who seem to always look for someone or something to blame when things don't go as planned? "It's the market. It's my supplier. It's the product. It's my boss." Accountability is the opposite of that. Being accountable means you make no excuses. You are accountable in every situation, and you are exactly where the buck stops.

Accountability has been considered a key element of Credibility for centuries. Greek philosophers Plato and Aristotle included the notion of accountability in their discussions of duty, justice, and punishment. But what does this word *accountability* mean? It is a complex topic, but let's see if we can make sense of it.

In order to understand how to be accountable, we first have to look at what accountability is. As you would imagine, we find a plethora of definitions that contain concepts that need explaining. In addition to truth and honesty, the qualities we find within accountability include: responsibility, answerability, justifiability and self-regulation. Thus, accountability is another *cluster concept*.

We also find some research into this topic, but most of it is academic and unusable. Let's think of accountability as the procedures and practices that guide your business behavior. This behavior must include responsibility to yourself, to your employer (or stakeholders) and to your client. Those elements enter into a dynamic relationship and become self-regulating. The problems mainly come when the employer/stakeholder side is vacant—as when you are an independent or self-employed person with no one for you to answer to other than the client and yourself. That's a formula for abuse.

Philip Tetlock is the researcher known for doing the most valuable work in this area. He suggested that "Accountability is the fundamental social contingency driving individuals' behaviors." He explained that people become accountable because they are concerned about their image and status, or because to be accountable (or not) brings an expectation of a potential evaluation—reward and/or punishment.

The rule for whether or not you are accountable comes from your promise, or guarantee, to your clients. The clients have needs and wants, and you have promised to satisfy them. If you fall short, you need to be accountable. Proving accountability up-front goes a long way toward establishing an expectation of Credibility in the mind of the client. If problems or disagreements ensue, your follow-up actions to take responsibility will likely maintain your Credibility. Neglect those follow-up actions and you lose your Credibility.

The Promise of Promises

Accountability is affected by the promises you make and your ability to keep them. That's not just rhetoric. Tony Simons, associate professor of management and organizational behavior at Cornell, confirms that keeping your promises has value to a company's bottom line. The Simons study involved 6500 employees from seventy-six companies in the hospitality industry. He found that an increase in score of only one-eighth of a point on a five-point scale in a hotel's behavioral integrity (consistency between words and actions) on employee surveys would improve the hotel's annual profits by 2.5 percent of revenues.

For an average full-service hotel, this is $261,000 added to the bottom line. "Hotels where employees strongly believed their managers followed though on promises and demonstrated the values they preached were substantially more profitable than those whose managers scored average or lower."

Being accountable for your promises means operating within the values and schedule of the client. Let's say you make a promise: "I will get this to you Monday." You'd better understand how the client interprets Monday. Is it start of business on Monday morning or close of business on Monday evening? This little detail becomes even more important when you're located in a different time zone from your client. We're in Washington state and thus three hours earlier than our clients on the east coast. When we're eating lunch, they're getting ready to drive home. If a project is promised for Monday morning, is it Eastern Time or Pacific Time? The answer, of course, is whatever the client says it is. For some of you, keeping promises is sometimes just a matter of better organization and a more effective calendar.

Humility

No one goes through life unscathed by embarrassment. No one can maneuver the obstacle course of adulthood without making some mistakes. How we handle ourselves in these uncomfortable situations helps to shape our Credibility.

Admitting Mistakes

We live in a culture that believes in and values perfection with little patience for mistakes. This belief breeds an expectation that everyone else should conform to our own view of what's right and appropriate. As absurd as that sounds for anyone over the age of six, we see it every day. I remember Lily Tomlin telling the joke,

"Being a New Yorker means never having to say you're sorry." If you have fallen into the trap of being reluctant to admit mistakes, you are sabotaging your own Credibility. Admitting and taking responsibility for mistakes can be powerful builders of Credibility and integrity. Mistakes are opportunities to visibly demonstrate a commitment to honesty and responsibility.

According to a survey in *Your Company* magazine (and quoted in *The Transparency Edge*), companies can get as much as 50 percent of their former customers back simply by picking up the phone and apologizing for past mistakes. Often, all it takes is a conversation in which a company representative apologizes for the blunder. It could be a late shipment, a typo on an order entry, or hundreds of other mistakes. The apology, which costs the company nothing, makes the customer feel valued, so he or she is more willing to return.

The message here is simple: taking responsibility and making yourself accountable has an impact on your bottom line. Failing or refusing to do that also has an impact on your bottom line, but it's not a good one.

Apology Bonuses

In 2001, Cisco, Intel, Dell and Nortel had to rescind job offers due to changes in the economy. Rather than just say "Sorry, things happen," these companies chose instead to protect their brand and reputation by giving "apology bonuses." Here is the story as reported by Matthew Boyle in *Fortune Magazine*, June 2001.

> FORTUNE. They're sorry. So sorry. After making job offers to a slew of college and MBA students from the class of '01, many belt-tightening employers—including Cisco, Dell, and Intel—have suddenly asked the grads to, uh, not come to work after all.

While some of the companies are giving their would-be hires nothing more than walking papers, several others are demonstrating their burning regret with cold, hard cash, offering so-called apology bonuses of up to three months' pay. Since the starting salary for engineers can hit $50,000 and MBAs generally make almost twice that, the consolation prizes can run over $10,000 a pop—not bad for someone who never even showed up at the office.

2. Competence

The second character trait of Credibility is Competence. Competence is the state or quality of being adequately or well qualified—having the ability to perform a specific role. Competence means you know how to do your job to the satisfaction of your client. We've entered into some heated discussions with some very bright people over the degree of competence that should be required and the relationship of competence to Credibility. The discussion always comes down to results, or what you do with your competence.

Clients want someone acting on their behalf to possess enough expertise to do their job successfully. If that's you, it doesn't necessarily mean that you need to be the world's leading expert, although that would be a nice added value. Nor do you necessarily need to have a PhD, MBA or whatever credentials are associated with the highest levels of your profession. The point is, credentials might add to your Credibility, but they do not create your Credibility. In fact, it's possible that a designation could hurt your Credibility. Research in the financial industry shows that credentials are only of value if the target market knows what those letters mean. A February 2007 *Business Week* article claims, "the financial-services world boasts nearly 90 designations, titles, degrees, affiliations,

119

certifications, and accreditations, some of which require little more than a check to obtain." The quantity of designations renders most of them meaningless.

As we discussed earlier regarding the three Levels of Credibility, there is a certain amount of perceived or assumed competence that comes with being a professional. As Harry Beckwith, author of *Selling the Invisible*, said, "In most professional services, you are not really selling expertise—because expertise is assumed, and because your prospect cannot intelligently evaluate your expertise anyway. Instead you are selling a relationship." Credibility is a level of trust bestowed on you and the person you are, not on your resume.

Is competence the same as Credibility?

In a word, no! Competence is an aspect of Credibility, but without integrity, relevance and results competence is meaningless. It's also meaningless unless and until you are able to communicate your competence to your clients in a way that is relevant and understandable to them.

Ever communicate with a scientist or someone who is a subject matter expert in a highly complex area? Alan Greenspan, former chairman of the Board of Governors of the Federal Reserve of the United States, is one of the most famous subject matter experts. His explanations were so confusing that the radio show Motley Fool used to play a call-in game called "What Did the Fed Chief Say." The point is, these people are often so knowledgeable that it's difficult for them to relate to how much normal people don't understand about the topic, and they are generally not driven to try to make what they're saying understandable to the layperson. This may not be harmful in some situations, but it most certainly is harmful in a sales situation. Here's what happens. When you can't understand what the other person is saying, there's no way for you to be certain that he is giving you truthful and relevant information. Red flags go up and you immediately become suspect of that person's Credibility.

The Importance of Being Understood

Research shows us that when your message is difficult to understand, your audience may believe that you are intentionally obfuscating the decision process in order to make it difficult to refute. In other words, you are purposely making your message or process difficult to understand to serve your own agenda.

Here's a great example. Studies by Elsbach, Sutton, and Principe suggest that patients believed hospitals purposefully made it difficult to challenge their bills by sending hard-to-read bills and implementing complex complaint-handling systems. This signaled to the patients that the hospitals were highly bureaucratic organizations and any challenges to bills would be futile.

Be jargon-free

The lexicon of industry terminology in your profession was developed for a specific reason. It's a type of shorthand for you inside your profession used to communicate with each other in a more efficient manner, but it is not intended to be used with your clients.

Research by Thompson et al. on the use of professional jargon shows that the more jargon-laden the language, the lower the overall rating of the speaker. Both expert and non-expert audiences rated believability lower when they encountered jargon.

Australian professors Joiner and Leveson looked specifically at the use of technical language by financial planners and advisors and its effect on their Credibility. Their conclusion is, "The challenge for the professional advisor is to provide useful advice without resorting to highly complex language and confusing the client. To the extent that the advisor can successfully accomplish this aim, the lay client is more likely to view the advisor as likeable, competent, worthy of trust, and more likely to engage the advisor's services."

It appears that people follow a hierarchy of processing to initially evaluate a message. In order, the criteria are: ease of comprehension, then personal relevance. If the message fails on both those points, the evaluator will look to secondary criteria: the expertise of the message source, and the legitimacy of the decision process. This was illustrated by Petty, Cacioppo & Heesacker in 1981. This tells us that we can take two giant steps toward ensuring a successful result by simply making sure our message is understandable and relevant.

3. Relevance

We've already talked about the process of evaluating the credibility of the message. The first step is understandability. The second is relevance. Let us ask here, just what exactly is relevance, and how do you know if your message is relevant?

Relevance is the extent to which what you are saying or presenting is meaningful to the other person. Relevance can be subjectively measured by determining how close your message is to what the prospect is actually interested in. In fact, you can picture this measurement by drawing a simple two-circle Venn diagram. One circle is you and

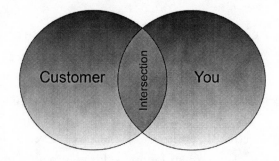

Figure 7-3: Intersecting Circles

122

what you represent. The other circle is the prospect and what he wants. How much do the circles overlap? For a perfect fit, they would look like only one circle. For no fit, there would be no overlap.

Example 1. Let's say the prospect is located in New Orleans and wants to protect an office building against the risk of weather-related damage. Topics related to hurricanes, storm surges, high tides and wind are where you would show your credibility. The farther you get from that topic, the less relevant you become. If you represent insurance for storm damage, then your circles would overlap. If you represent (for example) financial planning or home security, then the edges of your circles would not even touch.

Example 2. Let's say the prospect is a business owner who wants to retire after handing control of the business over to his son. Topics related to exit strategies, transition of control, key man training, business valuation and estate planning are where you would show your credibility. If you are there to discuss those topics, your circles would overlap. If you're there to represent, for example, office equipment or staff outsourcing, then the edges of your circles would not touch.

4. Objectivity

Objectivity plays a key role in both trust and credibility and is directly tied to your intent. In order to trust and believe what you have to say, I must believe that you are objective, not working your own agenda or locked in a particular point of view. Objectivity is related to honorable intentions, transparency and honesty. When you are objective, you put everything out on the table and trust the other person to decide the appropriateness of the fit. You are forthcoming with information, even information that may not support your particular product or platform.

In fact, one of the best ways to demonstrate credibility is to talk about the negative elements and disadvantages of, or to argue against, your own position. You gain Credibility when you appear objective looking at your own product, service, idea or opinion. Pointing out the negative also disarms the prospect from trying to find it himself, leaving him to focus on the benefits.

Kevin Hogan is his book *The Science of Influence*, reminds us that every great speaker knows that when you bring up the point of view that disagrees with your own you are more likely to win the audience over. Why? If that is what they are thinking, you defuse or inoculate your audience against the opposite point of view. The more you say that (positively) surprises your audience or client in this respect, the more likely you are to gain critical persuasion points.

Whether or not you should include arguments for and against your case depends very much on your prospects. If you know they already agree with you, a one-sided argument is OK. If they hold any opinion that differs from your point of view, then a one-sided message will actually be *less* effective and will be dismissed as biased.

Carl Hovland's investigations into mass propaganda used to change soldiers' attitudes also suggests that the intelligence of the receiver is an important factor, and that a two-sided argument tends to be more persuasive with the more intelligent audience.

5. Results

Credibility is not the result of an event, so it must be proactively maintained. The one thing that determines credibility more than any other is the result you generate for your client or customer. You can be competent, relevant, honest and well-intentioned, but if you do not produce results for your client, your credibility will not be sustainable. Results are the proof of your credibility.

It's not just the results themselves that count, it's the client's awareness of those results. Thus, it's important to be able to appropriately communicate results to others. In addition, it's not only today's results or yesterday's results that matter; it's the client's faith in your ability to produce future results that drives Credibility.

> *Our Credibility comes not only from our past results and our present results, but also from the degree of confidence others have in our ability to produce results in the future.*
>
> -- Stephen M.R. Covey—*The Speed of Trust*

Last Impressions— the Impact of Primacy and Recency

We've talked a lot about first impressions as regards both Likeability and Credibility. We've discussed the factors that contribute to the other person's first impression of you. First impressions are critically important, but so are last impressions. The order in which you and your message are presented to your audience impacts how they perceive you.

We know from the research that, if presented with a list of items, we will most likely remember the first few and the last few. In psychological terms, this is known as *cognitive bias*, and the science behind it is called *primacy effect* (we remember the first ones best) and *recency effect* (we remember the most recent ones).

Here's how it works. Primacy: At the beginning of a sequence of events (or list), the *long-term memory* is far less crowded. As you mentally review them, you rehearse number one, then numbers one and two. With each new item you review, you add the previous ones. Recency: the items still present in *working memory* and are easier to recall.

Here's how this plays out in the business world. Smart presenters seek to be the first or last one to present. Attorneys carefully order witnesses and put key witnesses at the end of the list or at the beginning to take advantage of these innate biases. When you make a presentation, don't you open with an intriguing or provocative statement to grab attention? That's primacy. Don't you close with a powerful statement that you want the audience or prospect to remember or act on? That's recency.

The other spot in this sequence is the intermediate position. Research shows that recall of information delivered in the middle of a sequence or list is greatly reduced. This is where you would put information that you did not place high value on.

What's more important?

One of our favorite authors is a political advisor named Dr. Frank Luntz. He wrote a fascinating book titled *Words That Work* in which he gives a great illustration of the importance of order or sequence in communication.

> The importance of the order in which information is presented hit home for me when I was working with Ross Perot during the 1992 presidential campaign. I had three videos to test: (1) a Perot biography; (2) testimonials of various people praising Perot and (3) Perot himself delivering a speech. I'd been showing the videos to focus groups in that order, but at the beginning of one session, I realized I'd failed to rewind the first two videotapes, so I was forced to begin the focus group with the tape of Perot himself talking. The results were stunning.

In every previous focus group, participants had fallen in love with Perot by the time they'd seen all three tapes in their particular order. No matter what negative information I threw at them, they could not be moved off their support. But now, when people were seeing the tapes in the opposite order, they were immediately skeptical of Perot's capabilities and claims, and abandoned him at the first negative information they heard. Unless and until you knew something about the man and his background, you would get the impression that his mental tray was not quite in a full, upright, and locked position.

Chapter 8:
How to Demonstrate Credibility

Think of a science experiment or a cooking demonstration. You can combine the ingredients any way you want, and the end result is your Credibility. The ingredients include things like the people and institutions you associate with, the quality and repetition of your message, the way you look and sound and the results you produce.

It has been our experience in business that the vast majority of professionals we've met are well-intentioned and competent. They *are* credible. The problem they bump into is that their target markets don't know that they're credible because these professionals have yet to learn how to demonstrate their credibility or call it to the attention of their clients. It is simply the difference between being and doing.

We're talking about the *perception* of Credibility. The hard reality is, you could be wonderfully credible and not appear that way. If your prospects and clients don't perceive you as credible, then, for all practical purposes, you're not credible. Conversely, we've all met people who had little or no credibility but were seen as paragons of credibility. We don't condone that type of theater, but we can learn from it.

- Point one: You absolutely must learn how to demonstrate your credibility, and thus build that perception in the mind of your client or target audience. Remember their perception is their reality.

- Point two: It's a whole lot easier to demonstrate credibility if you actually are credible.

Throughout the rest of this chapter we identify specific things you can do to improve (or prove) your credibility.

1. Help Clients Self-discover Your Credibility Prior to the First Meeting

Think about the assumptions and perceptions your target market has of you before they ever actually meet you in person. What do they know of you? Will your name sound familiar? Have they read about you in the paper, seen your articles, heard about you from friends and colleagues or driven by your office?

What can you do to help clients self-discover your credibility before they meet you?

We are very fortunate in our work because the majority of our clients have read our books and articles before meeting us. That means they already have a self-determined idea or perception of our credibility. That doesn't mean that we don't have to work to maintain that perception. It simply means that we get a head start because we've already put the advance messages out into the market. Thus, we set up a system through which our readers and clients learn about us on their own in advance of contacting us directly. When they call, we don't have to focus as much on first impressions or proving our credibility.

As an example, we received a call today from a prospect who said, "I've been reading your stuff for some time now. It's really good, not vague like so many other writers. It's stuff we can actually put into effect."

As a result of this prospect's *self-discovery*, we didn't have to deliver a pitch; we just said thanks.

If you're not so widely published, then you can still create credibility that will precede you. This can be as simple as giving clients something to read or review before the meeting, or it can be as complicated as a multi-contact, multi-media, sequential communication program (like wave marketing). We'll talk about this more in the Credibility Marketing section.

Leverage (or compensate for) Inherited Credibility

We talked earlier about the three Levels of Credibility—Personal, Professional, and Organizational—as illustrated in Figure 8-1. This is simply a schematic of the law of perception, and here's how it works. You inherit credibility or lack of credibility by virtue of your industry, profession or associations.

If you are lucky enough to work for a company held in high esteem, use it to your advantage! We've worked with several clients who work for companies who have been listed in *Best Places to Work* or written about positively in the press. If there has been positive press on your company or profession, save the article and use it as part of the information you give clients to help paint the picture of your credibility.

Figure 8-1: Inherited Credibility

If you're not so fortunate and your company or profession has suffered negative press, it is critically important to build up your personal credibility. If you have previously established your own credibility, you become insulated somewhat from the negative affects falling from the outer circles.

Throughout 2000 and most of 2001, I (PH) was the poster girl for credibility. I was a highly credible management consultant working on a methodology for valuing intangibles like knowledge and customer relationships. I participated in the development of a best selling book and was busy working on the accompanying methodology and toolkit that would help companies implement our program. Our work was ground breaking, global and impactful.

Then, in the span of weeks, my credibility went from five-star to zero stars. I had not changed. I was exactly the same person I had been. I had not made any mistakes or broken any laws. What changed was damage to those outer circles. I was working with Arthur Anderson, and one of the firms they used as an example of how to implement this innovative form of valuation was Enron. Get the picture? Even though my group at Anderson was not involved with any of the Enron shenanigans, our credibility took a major hit when Anderson's overall credibility took a hit. Association with Enron devastated Anderson's credibility, which in turn affected our project, which in term tarnished my credibility.

What did I do to deal with the damage to my credibility? Although I didn't proactively *sell* this relationship immediately after the debacle, I didn't hide it either. I knew my personal credibility was still intact and I looked for ways to use the experience and damage to my outer circles. I developed the concept of levels of credibility and began to help others deal with similar experiences. This transparency proved to be a significant credibility re-builder.

Damage Control

Use the three levels as a schematic to represent a simple Credibility Strategy. You might think of this as your Damage Control Strategy. If those two outer circles are in good standing, you need to focus on the innermost circle—you. If, on the other hand, those outer circles lack credibility, then you have to determine which circle is the weak link and either fix it or make a change.

Use the following table to help you organize your thoughts and determine what steps to take.

Level	Current Credibility Perception	What to do to Repair/Improve
You		
Profession		
Company		

Credibility Marketing

Credibility Marketing is marketing focused on developing a picture of your credibility in the minds of your target market. It capitalizes on three psychological elements: source credibility, source variability and familiarity.

Source Credibility

Think of all the different areas of your work. In which areas are you most credible? What proof or evidence do you have that backs up your claims of credibility? What type of tool (report, article, white paper, ad, book) might you use to communicate your credibility to your target market?

Source Variability

Remember, the more variable the sources, the better. That means variability in both the people who deliver your message and the delivery vehicle (book, article, ad, etc.) If you're mentioned in an article, that counts as one. If later you're recommended by a colleague, that's a second. Testimonials also help with source variability.

You'll also want to use different vehicles to deliver your message. For example, use a white paper followed by an article with excerpts from the article followed by a seminar on the same subject.

Familiarity

The more familiar people are with your message, the more likely they are to accept it. In the beginning, this is a passive process as the message is received, then it's considered. The process becomes proactive when it is recalled in the relevant context and applied. Credibility is awarded when the message is first accepted and then when the results are experienced.

For example, we've been publishing articles every month since 1986. When people read our work, they passively take in the message. The more often they experience it, the more anchored it is in their minds. At some point, when they need a solution that our work represents, our message will pop to the top of their minds as the most logical decision. They were open to it. They became comfortable with it as it became more familiar to them. Then they tried it and saw the results of using it.

When people come to our events, they are nearly always familiar with our writing. We've noticed that the vast majority of them relate to us as though we're old friends. They have developed a higher level of familiarity by having been repeatedly exposed to us.

Hierarchy of Marketing

When it comes to Credibility, not all Marketing elements are created equal. A book, for example, has more credibility power than a white paper, which is more powerful than an article, which is more powerful than a brochure. The Credibility Marketing Hierarchy looks something like this:

Book

TV Interview

Radio Interview

White Paper

Article

Presentation/speech

Newsletter

Website

Brochure

Direct Mail

Obviously the content of the book or article or the quality of the newsletter or brochure significantly impacts the perception of Credibility, but our focus here is just on the elements themselves.

The bottom line—if your focus is credibility, your time is better spent focused on the elements at the top of the list.

The biggest Credibility bang for the buck comes when someone else writes an article about you, or, better yet, a book about you. Remember our discussion of other messengers? This is psychologically significant in marketing as well. The more credible sources you can have talking about you or your product or service, the more credible the impression.

2. Employ Other Messengers

Sometimes another person can talk about you in a way that builds your credibility. People are far more likely to believe what someone else says about you than what you say about yourself. As Will Rogers said, "Get someone else to blow your horn and the sound will carry twice as far."

If you don't have the ear of the person who is important to you, find someone who does. If you have teenage kids, you might have realized that their soccer coach, band director or scout leader has more credibility than you do. Professionally, strangers are far more likely to believe what someone else says about you or your business than what you say.

That's a nice guideline, but how do you make it happen? Tell the other person what your message is, then help him or her feel comfortable delivering it. If you have to, engage in a practice session. For example, "Marisa, when you tell him about the consulting, here's what you can say…"

The key to effective use of the *other messenger* is to provide the messenger with information in a form that he or she can easily pass along. Make it an article, book, or brochure—something that says what you want to say and enables the messenger to easily add his or her two cents. We want to believe our messengers can figure out what to say on their own. We also tend to think that if we suggest they use a script that we're being pushy. The reality is, they probably could figure out what to say and how to say it, but they don't have the time, energy or incentive to focus on this. And why should they? Your job is to make it easy for other people to be your information messengers. Give them the tools they need to be effective at introducing you.

Example 1. One of our biggest corporate clients has a wholesaler who established a very promising alliance with a successful consultant. Unfortunately, every time the consultant tried to explain the wholesaler's product, he botched it. He was proving to be inept as a messenger. His heart was in the right place, but the rest of him was ill prepared for the task. What did the wholesaler do? He painstakingly taught the consultant how to talk about the product. The wholesaler gave the consultant content and worked with him to customize the content to fit his personal style. The result was a win-win-win. They wrote more business, and the consultant's clients were delighted with the results.

Example 2. On January 17, an article appeared in *Morningstar Advisor Magazine*. The subject was Pam and me. The columnist was David Drucker. He had called and interviewed us for the article, so we were able to give him concepts, ideas, and some specific language to explain them. David became our *other messenger*.

3. Get Credibility Introductions

One of our clients said, "Michael, it's not who you know that's important; it's how you know them."

In a one-on-one situation, get an introduction from someone with greater prestige, or someone whom the prospect already perceives as credible, or someone who has nothing to gain by saying nice things about you. The key to using the Credibility Introduction in a seminar situation is to find someone the audience will either like or trust. If that person can't improvise and think quickly on his feet, give him a basic script to follow. However, it's far better to use someone who can speak from the heart.

Example. Pam and I were recently introduced by one of our clients in the most credible and impactful ways we've ever heard. He said, "I want you to meet Michael and Pam. They have helped me tremendously and been instrumental in my credibility. Treat them like family—they're my A-team."

Not everyone can deliver an introduction like that. Most people need a script or talking points to follow. If you want to get credibility from an introduction, prepare talking points or a script for the other person to use, and work with him to make sure he is comfortable using it. That holds true no matter if you're being introduced at a networking event, neighborhood party or prior to your keynote. Carry an introduction typed out in large type with important words underlined and your name phonetically spelled out.

What someone else says about you (and how they say it) in an introduction determines how a new person will receive you. That's the first impression. Will he see you as just another salesman? Will he think of you as an amateur? You control that. Your personality is one thing, but your credibility and reputation are something completely different. You might be the life of the party or the most interesting guy in town, but when you are being introduced in a professional setting you need to be seen as a leader. That is exactly how your friends and business contacts need to position you when they introduce you. How would they know what to say? That's up to you.

Bottom line. You are automatically assumed to be more credible if a credible source recommends you or introduces you—and does it in the right way. When you introduce one of your vendors or alliance partners, he takes on some of your own credibility.

Now that you know it's important to use introductions intelligently, how can you structure an introduction to accomplish that? Let's say you're going to introduce someone else to open a seminar or teleconference:

- Think in terms of sound bites. That's a seven-second statement (30–40 words) intended to grab and hold the listener's attention for that short amount of time.

- Structure it in three areas: professional, personal and the closing.

- Deliver the most important and relevant sound bite first.

- Unless the audience is comprised of friends, never joke about the other person.

Professional Sound bite. I'd like to introduce a person who has been a role model to me for many years. His professional integrity serves as a beacon to advisors seeking to build careers on ethics and values.

Professional Sound bite. The author of eight books and a thousand articles, he is perhaps the best-known authority on Credibility and the psychology of communication in our industry today.

Personal Sound bite. They say the mark of a truly honest man is someone who is honest when he doesn't have to be. I've watched this person approach his personal life with the same depth of character we've seen him apply in business. For him, it seems, character never takes a day off.

Closing. Please join me in welcoming my friend—our speaker—Mr. Abe Lincoln.

4. Associate With Other Credible People and Associations

Throughout American history, the people seen around the president (or any other leader) have been afforded credibility (by association). The obvious thinking is, if the leader of the free world wants this person around, then she must be important or have some value. That's the essence of credibility by association. Think about pictures you've seen in people's offices showing them with important figures. I was in a client's office the other day and noticed a picture of him and President Bush. Even though I'm not a Bush fan, the Credibility power of that photograph is huge!

You don't have to be an associate of the president to achieve credibility by association. The leader could actually be a politician, CEO, military officer, or scout leader. It could be an author, speaker or religious leader. You might think about it like this—who is it that is held in high regard by the people I want to do business with?

Institutions also provide credibility by association. Let's say I offer to give you complete, all-expenses paid funding to get a graduate degree. You can go anywhere you want. Where would you go? The local university probably has the least credibility. The state university is better, but an Ivy League university would be even better. What if you could choose between The University of Phoenix (online degree program) and Harvard? Which one carries greater credibility? For the rest of your life, you would carry the association of that university. In spite of the many advantages the University of Phoenix offers, it doesn't compare to a world-class institution like Harvard.

In your industry, you represent your aggregate education too. If you have a university degree from a high-profile school plus quality professional credentials, you have mountains of credibility over someone who simply got a basic license and started making sales pitches. However, don't make the mistake of thinking that merely having those credentials will give you credibility. They won't. What they do for you is add to your overall Credibility Package.

It works on the flip side, too. If your employer has gotten a lot of bad press, that same tarnish rubs off on you. When I was preparing for a program that I was to deliver to a large financial firm, I asked what their people were most concerned about. One of their biggest concerns was how to maintain credibility while the company was under investigation by the Securities and Exchange Commission. Those people were experiencing loss of credibility by association.

As you probably already know, the answer to their puzzle was to have already built their credibility to the point where they were not negatively impacted by their association with the company.

Now let's switch gears and think about the specific people you associate with. Our friend Daniel Grissom, author of *STEP UP – How to Win More and Lose Less*, refers to this concept as *Buddying with the Best*. It stems from the recognition that we are judged by the company we keep. If we associate with high-integrity, credible people, others will assume that we have high integrity and are highly credible as well.

5. Cite Other Sources to Improve Legitimacy

One of the best ways to demonstrate personal credibility is by citing other (credible) sources to make the same point. This ties back to the psychological point we made earlier about familiarly. People are more likely to trust something they've heard about multiple times from multiple sources.

Many years ago, we began to incorporate some specific elements into our marketing programs. They included quotes from relevant publications along with the source citations. The idea was to find quotes that made our points for us, and to use the most credible sources we could find. We've since learned from research done by Feldman and March that there is great *legitimizing* power in the use of information sources. Here's how they say it:

> Legitimizing actions will affect perceptions of expertise and competence. Information use symbolizes a commitment to rational choice. Displaying the symbol reaffirms the importance of this social value and signals personal and organizational competence.

Borrow Credibility

How can you most effectively deliver information that is important to your target market? If you simply state it as your opinion, it doesn't carry much credibility. It will carry more power after you have established your credibility but not before. If, however, you cite quotes from third-party sources—ones that make the same points—you'll have communicated your information and gained credibility. Include some direct quotes, then cite the sources and the dates of publication. We call this *borrowing credibility*.

Imagine that your prospect wants to know if your suggestion is endorsed by anyone else. You have a choice: you could hand him a brochure from your firm, or you could hand him a stack of documents supporting your idea. They would include things such as articles from magazines, research papers, transcripts from panel discussions and interviews. What they would not include are sales magazines from your own industry or publications that are not recognized as objective and credible sources of information.

6. Look Credible

To business veterans, this might seem silly or obvious, but we include it here because we've seen too many people who arrive at meetings looking unkempt, scuffed and wrinkled, or wearing very strange combinations. Here are a few short examples:

- A CPA once arrived at one of our seminars wearing a dark blue suit coat with pinstripe pants. He looked like a mental patient.

- A Management Consultant we worked with was also an avid gardener. She told us about showing up for a business meeting and realizing midway through the meeting that she still had dirt under her fingernails.

- We once worked with a client whose favorite outfit was a gray suit, gray shirt and gray tie. He had a tendency to become invisible.

- When we lived in Texas, we had a client whose income relied on his conducting seminars. He was a dynamic, powerful person, but he insisted on wearing a pale yellow tie during his seminars. While his demeanor said *serious*, his tie said *wimp*. The incongruous combination damaged his credibility so much that audiences felt comfortable heckling him.

- Several years ago, JCPenney went from a formal everyday dress code to business casual. Unfortunately, the company did not teach its employees (the associates) what business casual looked like. As a result, a walk through the various departments would find associates wearing everything from worn-out jeans and sweatshirts to even more absurd mix-n-match combinations. The entire employee force was a functional definition of what credibility did not look like.

Your Objective. Make sure you're groomed and dressed appropriately. The trick is to understand what "appropriate" is, and the key to doing that is to understand the expectations of the person or people you will meet with. What do they accept and what do they reject?

Determine who it is that you want to make a positive impression on. Is it your boss, your client, your colleagues? Is it an audience or organization? Determine the level of their attire. Is it khakis and polo shirts, three-piece suits or jeans and leather jackets? Whatever it is, identify it, then build a wardrobe that is one step higher, or more serious, yet still appropriate. That is your look of Credibility. You'll find that when you dress one step higher, people will defer to you in conversations and your comments will be considered more seriously.

Let's look more deeply into this concept because if you apply it incorrectly, you'll lose credibility:

As a marketing writer during the 80s and 90s, I (ML) needed to dress conservatively, because the clients I met with were conservative, and I needed to show that I understood business. However, when I was going to meet with graphic designers or creative directors, I needed to prove I understood "taste." Thus, I needed to wear the most artistic tie I could find. That simple change bought me credibility with the two different types of people I dealt with.

Living in Texas for thirty years, we became sensitive to "outsiders" who came to meetings wearing a bolo tie and boots that were fresh from the western store. Those people were attempting to look the part and fit in, but they failed. They ended up looking phony, and there is no credibility in that.

In the past few years, as I've worked more and more with military veterans, I've made a radical change in my appearance. Most vets wear leather jackets and jeans. If I were to show up wearing a suit, I'd actually lose credibility. If I showed up wearing a brand new leather jacket and jeans, I'd lose credibility.

So, what are the explicit lessons here? Appropriateness is dictated by two things: 1) the different situations (or contexts) that you'll enter; and 2) the people you'll meet with. They determine how you will need to look.

7. Sound Credible

The sound of your voice has an effect on your perceived credibility. Our favorite example of this comes from the 1992 presidential campaign of Ross Perot. He was a brilliant guy with a horrible voice and it gave the late-night comedians a wealth of material. If you remember his high-pitched voice, use it as an example of what you do not want to sound like.

Pitch. There is a simple truth here. The lower your voice, the more credible you sound. There are people making lots of money serving as thought leaders to the world, and their main attribute is their voice. Think of the network TV news. For those times when you are called on to present your ideas, know how to lower the pitch of your voice.

My guess is that only people who are regularly recorded understand that they have multiple voices at their disposal. It was only last year that I (ML) discovered that I have a very deep, resonant voice I can call on when appropriate. It sounds like the announcer who introduces the TV show *Law & Order*. I discovered this voice when I was recording a radio show and the microphone was *hot*. I wanted to sound confident, but I had to lower the volume coming from me, otherwise the sound would have been distorted. The result was a surprising voice I'd never before heard come out of my mouth. I thought, "Who's in there?"

Volume. When you're presenting to a group, does your voice carry to the people in the back? If not, you have damaged your credibility with them. We live in a culture that includes many people who are hearing-impaired. That includes most of the seniors and boomers. It includes just about anyone who was ever in the military or listened to rock and roll. Whatever the cause, if you don't speak loud enough for them to hear you, they will simply tune you out. And that can't be good.

Speed. There is a perception that people who speak fast are more intelligent, and people who speak slowly are less intelligent. This has been a problem for people from the South for a hundred years. In terms of practicality, the middle ground is where you want to aim. It's the safest speed, but the real skill is in being able to speed up or slow down your rate of speech.

How can you do that? To slow down the speed of your speaking, lower the pitch and/or talk more softly. To speed up your speaking, raise the pitch and/or increase the volume.

We have many coaching clients who deliver seminars. We teach them to begin their program with the deepest, most resonant voice they can manage, then allow the voice to increase in both pitch and volume as appropriate and comfortable. When you need to emphasize points, go back to your low-slow voice. Speaking slowly helps other people process your ideas and remember what you say, but if you're not already seen as somewhat credible, speaking slowly could cause them to think you're not the brightest bulb in the box.

Damage control. Most of the smartest people you'll encounter in business are those who have an analytical personality type. Unfortunately, they often speak slowly because they are thinking while they're talking. In addition, these people think more deeply than others. It's like their minds are processing ten times more information than other people's do and giving only half enough energy to express it. Because their minds are preoccupied with thinking rather than presenting, they speak at a lower volume and slower speed.

What can you do? If you're analytical, try to plan ahead so you can present information you've already thought through. This will allow you to gain a confident grasp of the information, and that will speed up your delivery and add energy to your voice. If you're in a meeting with a slow-talking, analytical person, have patience. If you jump in or get exasperated with that type of delivery, you'll lose Credibility with that person, and he will have to start all over again.

8. Smell Credible

Consider the impression you give to other people through their senses. You work to look the part and know how to demonstrate your competence and relevance, so you have visual and auditory covered. You learn to shake hands with a firm, confident grip, so you have the kinesthetic covered. The other major sense that comes into play is olfactory—smell. The most important offenders of this sense are body odor, halitosis and cologne or perfume.

We understand that some people simply have unfortunate chemical reactions, which manifest in unfortunate odors from their person. What we don't understand are the people who drench themselves with liquids that give off strong odors. The rule with odors of choice is less is more and none is probably best. Smell is one thing you do not want to call attention to.

9. Be Jargon Free

Research cited in the previous chapter shows us that highly complex, jargon-filled techno-speak will actually detract from your credibility rather than add to it.

Think about your typical presentation. Write it out; then go back through it and circle the jargon or technical language. Sit down and write out how you might communicate the same information without using the technical terms. Look for metaphors, stories and anecdotes that make the point in a way that's easier for your prospects and clients to understand.

10. Point Out a Negative or Argue Against

Because individuals have specific needs, your product or service will not be perfect for everyone. With that in mind, you can gain credibility by pointing out a disadvantage or negative aspect of your product or service. You gain credibility when you appear objective when looking at your own product, service, idea or opinion. Pointing out the negative also disarms the prospect from trying to find it himself, leaving him to focus on the benefits.

In order to make sense of downplaying your own business, consider what a win for you might be. What could possibly be better than a sale? The answer is a referral. That's because a buyer might buy only one thing from you, but the source of the referral is likely to give referrals for years. Even if you have to sacrifice a sale, you put yourself in position to gain much more simply by being courageous enough to tell both sides of the truth.

11. Use Diagnostic Questions to Build Credibility

Many people make the mistake of declaring their credibility rather than letting the other person self-discover their credibility. The latter is far more effective. Asking intelligent and relevant questions is a great way to enable your client or prospect to do just that. Thomas A. Freese, in *Question-Based Selling* says:

> By demonstrating that you know how to ask intelligent and relevant questions, you communicate higher levels of competence, credibility and value. This automatically sets you apart from other sales people who either claim their own credibility or sound like they're reading from a script.

What kinds of questions? As salespeople, most of us have been taught to use open-ended questions to get people talking and involved in our conversation. Although these questions are important, when do you use them and what do you use them for?

The point is, before your prospects will trust you enough to start answering open-ended and highly personal questions, they must perceive you as credible and trustworthy. The bottom line is this: closed-ended, specific questions help you establish credibility, and they're easier for the prospect to answer.

In *Question-Based Selling*, Freese uses the story of a physician and patient to illustrate this point.

> Imagine you are a patient in a hospital and a physician comes in to check your condition—not your family doctor whom you have known for twenty years, but a specialist who was called in to perform a specific procedure. How would you react if the doctor came into your room and struck up a conversation by turning on a fake smile and asking, "So what are your medical goals and objectives for the next five years?" Most of us would feel a little uneasy. We might even question his competence or his sanity.
>
> As a patient, I would want my doctor to be the consummate professional. I would want him to initiate an intelligent dialogue by asking questions that would bolster my confidence and show me that he knows what he's doing. I would want him to ask if I was allergic to any medications. I would want him to ask questions about symptoms that I've been experiencing and about my medical history. The

more specific the questions the better, since each diagnostic question would raise my confidence that his understanding of the problem would help produce the best solution.

Begin with specific questions that show your credibility. These would be based on what and how. Then move systematically into more open-ended questions. Open-ended questions are based on why.

12. Help Clients Become More Discerning (so they can judge for themselves)

Clients are likely not good judges of your competence or expertise, but that doesn't matter. In many consulting and advisory situations, a typical client may not be in a position to adequately judge the competence of the person being considered for hire. That doesn't mean clients won't judge your competence, it simply means their judgments may not be valid.

What can you do in this situation? First, you can purposefully seek out discerning clients who are able to recognize competence. Second, you can help clients become more discerning by providing them with objective, third-party information that helps them make good decisions.

An example of a firm taking the first approach is Syms, a department store chain that sells discounted designer labels. They proactively seek out and market to discerning customers. Their slogan is "an educated customer is our best customer."

An example of the second approach is Jack Waymire, founder of the Paladin Registry and author of *Who's Watching Your Money?— The 17 Paladin Principles for Selecting a Financial Advisor*. The

Paladin Registry is a well-documented registry of highly credible financial advisors. Like Syms, Paladin advisors recognize that their best clients are those who are discerning enough to recognize the difference between them and their less credible counterparts. And they cover their bases in two ways: marketing directly to the educated, discerning market; and also contributing to the education of those less-knowledgeable about how to select a financial advisor. Waymire's book (written prior to his forming the Paladin Registry) is an objective and highly credible guide for consumers. Paladin advisors often provide Waymire's book to prospects so those prospects can self-discover the advisor's value.

13. Become More Credible

In the previous chapter we talked about the character of credibility or the personal attributes that enable you to sustain credibility over time. Let's take a look at what we can do to improve or maintain optimal status in each of these areas.

13-1. Tell the Truth

One of the more unusual ways to increase credibility is by telling the truth about how you make money. Take the initiative and answer the question before the client asks it. They want to know how you're paid, what you're paid, if there are hidden fees and if you'll actually end up costing them more money than you're worth. They want to know the relationship of price to quality if they place their trust in you.

For you, this is a gut-check issue. If you passively allow fees to hide, for example, in the *mice type* of a legal document, are you not in truth committing a sin of omission or obfuscation? Knowing that people will be paying fees they probably don't know about and can't understand is flirting with trickery. Can you live with that?

Openly show your prospect how you will profit from your business together. After all, he's going to be wondering about that anyway. You will gain credibility and eliminate the worry at the same time when you present the information up front. Think about it like this: when you address the issue up front, you are helping the client avoid an uncomfortable situation. It's an act of kindness.

A few years ago, we hired a financial advisor who did not explain the fees connected to our mutual funds. When we asked about them, he said that they were inconsequential and not to worry about them. His credibility immediately went down in our eyes because it was not his decision to make. It was entirely up to us to decide whether the fees were inconsequential or not. All he would have had to do was pick up the contract, hold it out to the side and say, "These documents are basically all the same. They're confusing. Let me point out a few things to you, and you can make the decision as to how important it is."

We live in a world where parity breeds competition, and advice is often a commodity. Cost often becomes the major decision factor. Many businesses hide fees, and the result is damaging to the credibility of the person, the firm and the entire industry.

Solution. If your business is a complex one, such as finance or technology, you need to explain the costs in the client's own lay language to make sure he understands what he is paying. You also need to explain what he's paying for. You might open this conversation by asking, "Would you like to know how people in this industry get paid?" Thus, explaining that the fees are not isolated to just you or your firm, but are industry wide.

13-2. Declare Your Good Intentions

To ensure that you demonstrate good intentions, get in the habit of asking yourself these questions:

- Do I genuinely want what's best for both of us, or do I really want to win regardless of what happens to the other party?

- Do I really believe it's possible to come up with a win-win solution?

- Do I really understand what constitutes a *win* for the client?

- Am I open to synergy and alternative solutions?

- If a *win-win* is not obvious, what will I do?

By simply developing the habit of making explicit what constitutes a win for you and a win for the other person, you demonstrate your honorable intentions, and you take a giant step into the congruence that makes Credibility possible.

Stephen M.R. Covey in *The Speed of Trust* offers a second step toward demonstrating good intentions. It's called declaring your intent. He describes it this way:

> At some point early on in one of your first meetings, you will be faced with answering the questions of what you're able to do for the prospect. This is the time to be open and honest. This is especially pertinent when you're talking about your strengths and results. Let your clients know why you're sharing that information with them—that it's not bragging. Tell them that you're letting them know what is possible. You're seeking to gain their confidence that you have the abilities and track record to serve

them well. Declaring your intent and expressing your agenda and motives is likely to be a refreshing change for the client. It's a way to establish trust in the new relationship.

13-3. Demonstrate Accountability

Ever make a mistake? What did you do then to make it right? Most people do nothing—that's not accountability. People who understand accountability take care of the mistake and do whatever is necessary to make it right. One of the things they do is apologize to the person(s) affected. An apology with low accountability sounds like this, "OK, I'm sorry! There I said it. Satisfied?" An apology with high accountability sounds very different. It actually has three separate parts: apology for the blunder, what you'll do in the short term to make it right, and what you'll do in the long term to keep it from happening again.

- First—acknowledge. I want to apologize for missing the deadline. It was a mistake and I regret it.

- Second—short term. Let me make it up to you in the short term by working over the weekend.

- Third—long term. In the future, if any circumstances cause me to miss another deadline, I will forfeit a week's pay.

Accountability is simple and extremely easy—until you make a mistake. Then it's complicated and extremely difficult, or it would be if you did not have this process to guide you in how to make things right and soothe the situation.

13-4. Be Responsive

In 2008 a study was released by the LRN-RAND Center for Corporate Ethics, Law, and Governance. This study is titled "Investor and Industry Perspectives on Investment Advisers and Broker-Dealers," and it illustrates the disconnect between investors and their investment advisors. The number one negative comment about advisors was their lack of accessibility or attentiveness. Even though this study looked specifically at Financial Advisors, our experience suggests that responsiveness and attention are issues in all industries.

Solution. Demonstrate your responsiveness during your first meeting with a client. We advise our clients to pull out their business card in front of the client and write their cell number on it while saying, "This is my personal number where you can reach me at any hour of the day, just in case you have any questions." This is a serious decision point for you. Do you really want to be available like that to your clients? This approach combines accountability and responsiveness to give you credibility. How you handle the calls will determine if you can keep that credibility.

13-5. Deliver Bad News Well

Into every client's life a little rain must fall. Your ability to deliver the news about that rain, and do it appropriately, shows your accountability. Consider that many people either blurt it out or pass the buck. That's not accountable or responsible, so how can you deliver bad news in an appropriate way?

When you have good news and bad news, deliver the good news first. When you have only bad news, begin by delivering the information that leads up to the bad news. The idea is to soften the blow because to do it in reverse causes the listener to pop into a different emotional state, one that makes listening difficult.

What constitutes bad news? Any time the information or decision is something different than the expectation of the person or people who will be affected by it, that is bad news. Any time you have to reject a project, turn down a request or otherwise say, "The decision is different from what you had expected," that's bad news.

Let's say you need to layoff an employee. If you say, "I have to let you go, and here's why..." The employee will be in shock and won't listen after the opening sentence. That is not only cruel, it is a recipe for resentment. That's not an appropriate way to handle that situation. However, if you lead with the reasons for the decision, you can handle the situation much more gracefully: "Steve, the economic downturn has caused our customers to stop buying our products. The company has reduced the budget in our department, and I have some very hard decisions to make. I'm very sorry, but I'm going to have to let you go." See the difference?

14. Polish Other First Impression Elements

First Impressions: Your Office

As Credibility consultants, Pam and I have visited many offices with an eye on the first impression. What does the décor say about the person whose office it is? If you were the next $10 million client, would you feel comfortable in your own environment, or would you walk out?

An office environment is a stage, and the person designing the environment needs to think like a set designer. Picture a bare space with bare walls and concrete floor. Add a desk and a computer and you're in business, but who would feel comfortable there?

What would you have to do to turn that environment from retro-warehouse to boutique and business?

See yourself walking into an office and thinking to yourself, "Wow, this is really nice." What do you see, hear, feel and smell? What kinds of rugs are on the floor? How do they feel under your feet? What kind of art is on the wall? Are the pictures framed? What style of lamps and tables do you see, and is the light harsh or soothing? What do you smell? Is it burned coffee or fresh chocolate chip cookies?

Now comes the next step. Someone greets you and graciously offers you a cup of coffee, but when it arrives, you're handed a Styrofoam cup. Doesn't that shatter the illusion? Doesn't it imply that you're as disposable as the Styrofoam? Your office environment should make any visitor the star in a play about the ultra successful. It needs to be designed around making them feel extremely comfortable and special, so go to a discount home furnishings store and buy some nice crystal or china. If you want people to come back, make your office environment comfortable and inviting.

Banks and law firms use Doric columns to symbolize longevity. Accountants dress carefully and conservatively by conscious design to communicate they are methodical and attentive to detail. Investment firms use leather portfolios to symbolize prosperity. Ad agencies and marketing firms show awards and examples of their creative expression. Consciously or subconsciously these people are managing first impressions to raise the level of the clients' expectations.

First Impressions: Your Marketing Materials

Anyone in business has seen a thousand brochures, thus we all have expectations and comparisons in our minds. If your marketing materials don't fall within that range, you lose credibility. What makes any marketing piece credible? Mainly two things: the look and the content.

The look. They are clean, simple and professionally produced. That doesn't mean you have to pay big bucks to an advertising agency or marketing firm. It simply means the materials need to have the appearance of professionalism. You don't want a brochure to look like you wrote and designed it yourself and printed it out on your ink-jet printer. This means no clip art, cutesy pictures or curly cue fonts. Err on the side of conservatism in your selection of fonts, colors and illustrations.

For marketing, the most credible colors are royal colors—dark blue, burgundy, gold and dark green. For your business cards and letterhead, it's the opposite. In the early nineties, I (ML) conducted some primary research into the color of credibility. I wanted to know which color of letterhead would give the best impression of Credibility. The result was that bright white was seen by far as the most credible color for stationary. This is important to you because when someone looks at a document on your letterhead, she is actually taken into a temporary environment dominated by that color. The page comprises the majority of the reader's field of vision, thus it's like stepping into a room whose walls are painted in that color. What does the color of your letterhead say about you?

The most credible fonts depend on the message. If your message says that you're new and forward thinking, then you would use a *sans serif* font like Calibri. If your message says that you're solid and time-tested, then you would use a traditional font like Garamond or Times Roman. You would likely never use a novelty font—unless you manage a clown service.

The content. Why does anyone look at any marketing piece? To get information. People don't pick up your brochure looking for reading enjoyment. They want to know what you can do for them, and they want to know immediately. If they can't find that information quickly, they get weary and move on to something else. The flow of your information needs to follow a simple formula: the most important information goes first. Your firm's history is not important. Your bio is not important. What you can do for your chosen target market is important. What sets you apart from others is important.

In addition to the look and content of the message, the choice of vehicle or medium that carries the message also has an affect on the perceived credibility. A book carries more credibility than a report or white paper. Those items carry more credibility than a brochure. Factual, research-based information carries more credibility than the same content expressed as marketing copy, a web log or even a magazine article. Being listed as the author of an article carries more credibility than merely being quoted in one. Writing an industry-specific article carries more Credibility than writing a general (generic) one. The closer you can get to communicating with one individual person, the more credibility your marketing will carry for that person or people like him.

First Impressions: Your Website

In this day and age your website is critically important. This is true even if you don't actually get business from website visitors. Why? Because your website is a credibility tool. The reality is, we judge people and companies by many different variables. When we haven't yet met them and are forming a first impression, one of the places we go is their website. Knowing that, what sort of impression does your website give? What does it say about your professionalism, sophistication and credibility?

Let's look at this in two parts beginning with first impressions, then digging deeper into specific content.

Split-Second Impressions

We are often asked to critique professional websites. One of the most common mistakes we see is that the site assumes a visitor will read and believe every word. The most vital information is typically obscured amid an avalanche of words in long paragraphs. That's simply annoying to the visitor and it's seriously counterproductive. By the time the visitor finds the first vital fact, the first impression has already been made. If that person had to dig for your information, he or she is not impressed.

What is the smallest amount of time required for visitors to form impressions of websites? According to Gitte Lindgaard of Carleton University in Ottawa, the answer is fifty milliseconds! As described in an article in the scientific journal *Nature*:

> Lindgaard and her team presented volunteers with the briefest glimpses of web pages previously rated as being either easy on the eye or particularly jarring, and asked them to rate the websites on a sliding scale of visual appeal. Even though the images flashed up for just 50 milliseconds, roughly the duration of a single frame of standard television footage, their verdicts tallied well with judgments made after a longer period of scrutiny.

Lindgaard warns, "Unless the first impression is favorable, visitors will be out of your site before they even know that you might be offering more than your competitors."

What Are People Looking At?

What goes into those first impressions? What are people using to decide whether your website (and consequently you) are credible?

Professionalism. Does your site look like it was professionally done, or is it obvious that you and your teenage nephew put it together one Saturday afternoon? Does it look amazingly like dozens of other sites in your industry?

Congruence: Is your site congruent with your profession, industry and the expectations of your visitors? An ad agency site would look different from an engineer's site, which would look different from an estate-planning attorney's site. Know your market and the types of images, color, and content that appeals to it.

Make sure the graphics and language on your site are congruent with your intention. Imagine our website, www.aboutpeople.com, without either pictures of people or content about understanding and relating to people.

What Elements of Your Website Enhance Your Credibility?

In our research into what builds credibility, we identified the top five content elements that affect credibility on a website:

1. Testimonials

2. Articles *about* you

3. Articles written *by* you

4. Associations and strategic alliances

5. Third-party references and research
   (capitalizing on the concept of *who else says so*)

In our digitized world, where anyone with a sixth-grade education can publish opinion, we must look at web content with a very skeptical eye and constantly ask for references and substantiation. Those tools listed above are the ones we've found to be the most effective at calming the skeptical eye of people looking at your website.

Chapter 9:
Trust Is Key to Maintaining Influence

In the beginning of this book, we taught you how to show people that you are safe and in that way help them learn to trust you. You learned that trust, or more accurately safety, is the first step in the process of Credibility and Likeability. Trust is more encompassing than just safety. Not only is trust important when people are forming initial impressions, it is also important in maintaining your influence once people decide they like you and find you credible.

You might think of trust as your Credibility and Likeability barometer. Which way is your trust arrow pointing? If it's pointing up, then you're building Credibility and Likeability. If you feel it starting to point down, you have some work to do.

Trust is a key element that requires your attention throughout the relationship. If you lose trust, it doesn't matter whether you are likeable or credible, you will likely damage, if not destroy, the relationship.

Stephen M.R. Covey, in his outstanding book *The Speed of Trust*, helps us understand the economics of trust. His book offers hard evidence on the bottom-line impact of trust. The simplified version of this is that trust affects two outcomes: speed and cost. When trust goes down, speed will also go down and costs will go up. Conversely, when trust goes up, speed will go up and costs will go down.

↓ Trust = ↓ Speed ↑ Cost
↑ Trust = ↑ Speed ↓ Cost

What is trust? Trust is simply a result. It's the result of your success in proving that you are congruent; that you can be relied upon to behave in a consistent and predictable manner; that you can be depended on to honor your commitments. But it's short-lived, meaning you have to continually reestablish it.

How do people decide if they can trust you? There are several levels of trust. As we discussed in the First Impressions section, the first level of trust is safety. Here's how it works:

- When I first meet you, my *trust detector* goes into action, and I decide if you are safe. This is my first look at trust.

- If I think you're safe, I'll check to see if you are respectful. Do you respect other people or just yourself? If you pass this test, I'll give you a tiny bit more trust.

- I'll look at you and listen to you looking for congruence. Do your actions and your words say the same things? If they are congruent, I'll give you a little more trust.

- I'll look at dependability. Will you look out for me and keep your word? If I decide you are dependable, I will give you even more trust.

- The highest level of trust is values-based trust. If we share the same values and I have seen congruence and dependability over time, our relationship can evolve into a much higher *without questions* level of trust.

The Trust pyramid looks like this.

Values Connection

Dependability

Congruence

Respect

Safety

Real trust is built over time but constantly is checked and double-checked throughout the process. Some of the things that people intuitively look for to determine whether they can trust you are:

- Safety

- Respect

- Congruence

- Consistency

- Dependability

- Values Connection

Safety

Safety is an unconscious mental process that takes place in the minds of your prospect. The ultimate question is: are you a danger to life, identity, beliefs, values, activities or security.

Respect

In order for your clients to trust you, they must believe you respect them. This means you:

- Respect their time. You keep your time commitments. You're there when you say you're going to be there and you end conversations and meetings on time.

- Respect their ideas. If you interrupt your clients, finish their sentences or jump to conclusions, you show that you do not respect their ideas.

- Respect their values. Be sensitive to religious beliefs, politics, ethnicity and any and all viewpoints and beliefs. Remove from your language and behavior all words and actions that your client might find offensive or invasive.

Congruence and Consistency

Congruence is one of the most important keys to creating trust. Congruence equals integrity. Congruence means:

- You are who you say you are.

- Your beliefs are appropriate and consistent.

- You take action on your values, thus making decisions of integrity.

- Your behaviors and activities are based on your values.

- Your promises are based on your abilities and competencies.

- You don't promise what you can't deliver.

As Harry Beckwith says in *Selling the Invisible,* "Prospects do not buy how good you are at what you do. They buy how good you are at who you are." Consistency means you can be depended on to be congruent across multiple contexts and different types of situations.

You believe in what you're doing. You can't expect a prospect to believe in you, and therefore trust you, unless it is clear that you genuinely believe in the following: what you're doing, the products you provide, services you render, the advice you give and the people you do business with. If you believe it, chances are, your prospect will as well. If you have doubts about what you're doing—change it.

Dependability

Now that you have shown that you can be trusted, at least initially, how do you move to the next level of trust, which is based on dependability? You establish this level of trust when clients trust you to do something and you deliver according to (or exceeding) their expectations.

Values Connection

The deepest level of trust comes when you make a values connection. That means you share the same values and act in accordance with those values in your work together. Values drive our decisions and behaviors. If you share values with a client, it will likely mean that you tend to make the same kinds of decisions and engage in the same activities. That *connection* helps build a high level of trust. The deeper the values connection you have, the deeper and more sustainable the trust.

In Conclusion

Pam and I live our professional
lives with a belief that we are
truth facilitators. We find it,
organize it and then share
it through our teaching and
publishing. Thing is, the finding
never stops. We are continually
adding to and improving what
we've discovered. This book captures a portrait of today's truth. As
we find more truths, we will share them through our articles and in
our training. Of course, we'll also include them in the next edition
of this book.

What will those new truths be? My guess is they'll include ways you
can become even more accurate and effective at building credibility
and becoming more likeable. I know we'll discover ever more
effective psychology to inspire other people.

This book has taken us all many giant steps down a path few people
have ever explored. It has been said that nothing great is ever

accomplished without passion. It should be obvious that Pam and I live passionately about this topic. We didn't just sit down one day and write this book. It has been a work in progress since 1991. It takes a lot of passion to continue any journey for that long!

Our journey has caused us to seek out more and more education in psychology—the psychology of communication, psychology of business relationships, psychology of learning. Those are the essential skill sets that make business possible. It's taken years to gain this understanding and learn the skills, but each lesson is a step in this never-ending journey to find and share truth.

If you look around your industry, you will likely find that most professionals sleepwalk through their careers, not knowing how to demonstrate their credibility or help people like them. Their results ultimately reflect that inability. They always come to the same false conclusion—that they need help with prospecting. If they would build their credibility and make themselves more likeable, they'd get more referrals and prospects would seek them out.

If you implement the advice in this book, you will see a change in your business. You'll see people relate to you in a different way. You'll see the change in the way they look at you and how they treat you. It is a humbling experience. That is what Pam and I want for you. If we can be of help to you, just contact us through our website: www.aboutpeople.com

Appendix A:
The Credibility Index

In July of 1999 the findings were released from a fascinating survey released by the Public Relations Society of America (PRSA). The research involved several thousand in-depth interviews and produced an index that rates professions according to their perceived credibility.

Professional athletes fared very badly, but they outranked political party leaders, PR specialists, entertainers and TV-radio talk show hosts—who ranked last. Can you see why? All those people have an agenda. Why would you trust someone whose goal it is to satisfy his or her own personal objectives instead of yours? Flatly, you wouldn't, and thousands of people indicated that in this survey.

The research team spent five years on this survey and produced 5,000 pages of material. The team found that credibility was complex and full of intangibles: demographics, attitudes, peer influence, life experience, ideology and civic involvement. Essentially what it means is that for a spokesperson to be seen as credible, he or she must be perceived as honest, competent and a leader.

The following is the order of credibility as determined by several-thousand Americans. Where would you rate yourself?

1. Supreme Court justice
2. Teacher
3. National expert
4. Member of the armed forces
5. Local business owner
6. Ordinary citizen
7. Local religious leader
8. High-ranking military officer
9. School official
10. National leader with shared traits
11. National religious leader
12. Network TV news anchor
13. Governor
14. Local business representative
15. Local newspaper or TV reporter
16. National civil rights leader
17. Locally elected council member
18. U.S. senator
19. Nationally syndicated columnist
20. Mayor of a big city
21. Head of state-level agency
22. Head of a local-level agency
23. Reporter for large newspaper or magazine
24. U.S. congressman
25. Head of a large corporation
26. National Credibility Index
27. Local civil rights leader
28. U.S. vice president
29. Head of national association
30. Community activist
31. Wall Street executive
32. Head of a presidential advisory board
33. U.S. president
34. Member of presidential Cabinet
35. Pollster
36. Student activist
37. Local labor union leader
38. Candidate for public office
39. Head of national labor union
40. Famous athlete
41. Head of national interest group
42. Political party leader
43. Public relations specialist
44. Famous entertainer
45. TV or radio talk show host

Bibliography

Anthony, Mitch. *Selling with Emotional Intelligence*. Kaplan Publishing, 2003.

Armstrong, J. Scott. 2008. Predicting Elections from Politician's Faces. The Wharton School, University of Pennsylvania.

Bailenson, Jeremy N., Shanto Iyengar and Nick Yee. 2007. Facial Similarity between Voters and Candidates Causes Social Influence. Stanford University Department of Communication. Soon to be published by *Public Opinion Quarterly*.

Bickman, Leonard. 1974. The social power of a uniform. *Journal of Applied Social Psychology*.

Blake, Kenneth R. and Robert O. Wyatt. Has newspaper credibility mattered? A perspective on media credibility debate. *Newspaper Research Journal*, Winter 2002.

Boyle, Matthew. 2001. Take That Apology and Spend It. *Fortune*. http://money.cnn.com/magazines/fortune/fortune_archive/2001/06/11/304595/index.htm

Brooks, Bill and Tom Travisano. *You're Working Too Hard to Make the Sale*. Irwin Publishing, 1995.

Bryner, Jeanna. 2008. Marketing the Next President of the United States. *Live Science*. http://www.livescience.com/history/080201-candidates-marketing.html

Casciaro, Tiziana and Miguel Sousa Lobo. 2005. Fool vs. Jerk: Whom Would You Hire? *Harvard Business School Working Knowledge Newsletter* 83.

Cialdini, Robert B. *Influence: The Psychology of Persuasion*. New York: HarperCollins, 1999.

Cohen, Geoffrey. 2003. Party over Policy: The Dominating Impact of Group Influence on Political Beliefs. *Journal of Personality and Social Psychology* 85: 808–822.

Conger, Jay. The Necessary Art of Persuasion. *Harvard Business Review OnPoint*, 2000.

Covey, Stephen, and Rebecca Merrill. *The Speed of Trust*. New York: Free Press, 2006.

DeBruine, Lisa. 2005. Trustworthy but not lust-worthy: context-specific effects of facial resemblance. *Proceedings of the Royal Society of London B* 272: 919–922.

Dutton, D.G. & Aron, A.P. 1974. Some evidence for heightened sexual attraction under conditions of high anxiety. *Journal of Personality and Social Psychology*, 30, 510-517.

Eldeman, Global Opinion Leaders Study, 2006. http://www.edelman.com/trust/2008/

Elsbach, K.D. & G. Elofson. 2000. How the Packaging of Decision Explanations Affects Perceptions of Trustworthiness. *Academy of Management Journal* 43: 80–89.

Elmer, Eddy M. and Jim Houran. 2008. Physical Attractiveness in the Workplace. *Hotel News Resource.* http://www.hotelnewsresource.com/article31439.html

Feingold, Alan. 1992. Good-looking people are not what we think. *Psychological Bulletin* 111: 304–341.

Feldman, Martha S. and James G. March. 1981. Information in Organizations as Signal and Symbol. *Administrative Science Quarterly* 26:171-186.

Gerbert, Barbara. Perceived likeability and competence of simulated patients: influence on physician's management plans. *Social Science & Medicine,* 1984.

Goleman, Daniel, Richard E. Boyatzis and Annie McKee. *Primal Leadership: Learning to Lead with Emotional Intelligence.* Harvard Business School Press, 2002.

Grinder, John. Interview with John Grinder, July 1996, Boulder Colorado NLP Comprehensive http://www.inspiritive.com.au/grinterv.htm

Handwerk, Brian. 2005. A "Competent" Face Helps Win Elections, Study Suggests. *National Geographic News.* http://news.nationalgeographic.com/news/2005/06/0609_050609_elections.html

Heesacker, Martin, Richard E. Petty and John T. Cacioppo. Field dependence and attitude change: Source credibility can alter persuasion by affecting message-relevant thinking. *Journal of Personality,* April 2006.

Hellström, Åke and Joseph Tekle. 1993. Person perception through facial photographs: Effects of glasses, hair, and beard on judgments of occupation and personal qualities. *European Journal of Social Psychology* 24: 693–705.

Hopkin, Michael. Web users judge sites in the blink of an eye. Nature. com, January 2006.

Hogan, Kevin. *The Science of Influence. How to Get Anyone to Say "Yes" in 8 Minutes of Less!* Wiley Press, 2004.

Insight Magazine. 2007. Washington Watch: The Likeability factor: Hillary does not have it. *Insight.* http://www.insightmag.com/ ME2/dirmodasp?sid=&nm=Free+Access&type=Publishing&m od=Publications%3A%3AArticle&mid=8F3A702742184197 8F18BE895F87F791&tier=4&id=85FA52EC81294C5CB828 D391D65CF06C.

Joiner, Therese A. and Lynne Leveson. 2006. Financial Planner Credibility: the importance of being understood. *International Journal of Financial Services Management* 1: 438–449.

Jones, Ben. 2008. Perceiving Beauty. *Society Now.* http://www. esrcsocietytoday.ac.uk/ESRCInfoCentre/about/CI/CP/ societynow/Issue1/perceivingbeauty.aspx?ComponentId=28285 &SourcePageId=28341

Keating Caroline F., David W. Randall, Timothy Kendrick and Katharine A. Gutshall. 2003. Do Babyfaced Adults Receive More Help? The (Cross Cultural) Case of the Lost Resume. *Journal of Nonverbal Behavior* 27: 89–109.

Kouzes, James S. and Posner, Barry Z. *Credibility: How Leaders Gain and Lose it, Why People Demand It.* San Francisco: Jossey-Bass, 2005.

Lawrence, S. and M. Watson. (1991) Getting others to help: The effectiveness of professional uniforms in charitable fund raising. *Journal of Applied Communication Research,* 19, 170-185.

Luntz, Frank. *Words that Work: It's Not What You Say, It's What People Hear.* New York: Hyperion, 2008.

Lyon, Cody. 2006. Southern accents still come on strong. Ya'll got a problem with that?. *Columbia News Service*. http://jscms.jrn. columbia.edu/cns/2006-05-02/lyon-southernaccents

Maister, David H., Charles H. Green and Robert M. Galford. *The Trusted Advisor*. New York: The Free Press, 2001.

Martin, Nicole. 2008. Popularity is key to success. *UK Telegraph*.

Mehrabian, Albert. *Silent Messges*. Wadsworth, 1971.

Orwell, George. Politics and the English Language, 1946.

Reynolds, D'Arcy J. and Robert Gifford. The Sounds and Sights of Intelligence: A Lens Model Channel Analysis. *Journal of Personality and Social Psychology*, February 2001.

Pagano, Barbara and Elizabeth Pagano. *The Transparency EDGE – How Credibility Can Make or Break You in Business*. McGraw-Hill, October 2003.

PBS Special – The American Experience – Jimmy Carter http://www.pbs.org/wgbh/amex/carter/peopleevents/e_malaise.html

Preston, Dennis. Some Plain Facts about Americans and Their Language. *American Speech* – Volume 75, Number 4, Winter 2000, pp.398-401

Reed, J. Ann and Elizabeth Blunk. The influence of facial hair on impression formation. *Social Behavior and Personality: an International Journal*, February 1990.

Rinalducci, Ned. 2007. The effects of figurative language on the perceived credibility of political candidates. *Human Communication Research* 1: 75-80.

Roggeveen, Anne L. and Gita Venkataramani Johar. Perceived Source Variability Versus Familiarity: Testing Competing Explanations for the Truth Effect. *Journal of Consumer Psychology*, 12(2), 81-91, 2002.

Romano, Andrew. 2008. The Likeability Factor. *Newsweek*. http://blog.newsweek.com/blogs/stumper/archive/2008/10/08/the-likability-factor.aspx?print=true

Romano, S.T. and J.E. Bordieri. 1989. Physical Attractiveness, Stereotypes and Students' Perceptions of College Professors. *Psychological Reports* 64: 1099-1102.

Rule, Nicholas O. and Nalini Ambady. 2008. The Face of Success: Inferences From Chief Executive Officers' Appearance Predict Company Profits. *Psychological Science* 19:109–111.

Sanders, Tim. *The Likeability Factor: How to Boost Your L-Factor and Achieve Your Life's Dreams*. New York: Three Rivers Press, 2006.

Schneider, Bill. You don't have to be liked to be president…but it helps. CNN.com http://www.cnn.com/2007/POLITICS/06/13/schneider.likability/index.html

Satir, Virginia M. *The New Peoplemaking*. New York: Science and Behavior Books, Inc., 1988

Simons, Tony. 2002. The High Cost of Lost Trust. *Harvard Business Online*. http://harvardbusinessonline.hbsp.harvard.edu/b02/en/common/item_detail.jhtml?id=F0209A

Snow, Kate. 2008. Clinton Gets Emotional on Campaign Trail. *ABC News Blog*. http://blogs.abcnews.com/politicalradar/2008/01/clinton-gets-em.html

Sorokin, P.A. and J.W. Boldyreff. An Experimental Study of the Influence of Suggestion on the Discrimination and the Valuation of People. *American Journal of Sociology*, XXXVII (1932), 720-737.

Stephenson, Karen. 1998. What Knowledge Tears Apart, Networks Make Whole. *Internal Communications Focus* 36.

Tahmincioglu, Eve. 2007. Power of attraction rules in workplace: Good-looking bosses considered more competent, MSNBC survey finds. *MSNBC*. http://www.msnbc.msn.com/id/17369873/

Tetlock, Philip. Accountability in Social Systems: A Psychological Perspective. *Accountability for Criminal Justice – Selected Essays*. Edited by Philip C. Stenning. University of Toronto Press, 1995.

Thompson, Pat A. Jargon and Data Do Make a Difference. American Institute for Research, 1981.

Todorov, Alexander, Anesu N. Mandisodza, Amir Goren and Crystal C. Hall. 2005. Inferences of Competence from Faces Predict Election Outcomes. *Science* 308:1623–1626.

Todorov, Alexander and Janine Willis. 2006. First Impressions. Making Up Your Mind After a 100-Ms Exposure to a Face. *Psychological Science* 17:592–598.

Todorov, Alexander, Andrew D. Engell and James V. Haxby. 2007. Implicit Trustworthiness Decisions: Automatic Coding of Face Properties in the Human Amygdala. *Journal of Cognitive Neuroscience* 19:1508–1519.

Vince, Gaia. 2005. Voters give thumbs-down to baby-faced politicians. *New Scientist*. http://www.newscientist.com/article/dn7502

Weston, Drew. *The Political Brain*. New York: Public Affairs, 2008.

Yoon, Lisa. 2003. Survey: Honesty Still Highly Ranked Policy. CFO. http://www.cfo.com/article.cfm/3007930

Zajonc, R. B. 1968. Attitudinal Effects of Mere Exposure. *Journal of Personality and Social Psychology* 9: 1-27.

Zebrowitz, Leslie A. and Mary Ann Collins. 1997. Accurate Social Perception at Zero Acquaintance: The Affordances of a Gibsonian Approach. *Personality and Social Psychology Review* 1: 204-223.

Zebrowitz, Leslie A. 2001. Looking Smart and Looking Good: Facial Cues to Intelligence and Their Origins. *Personality and Social Psychology Bulletin* 28:238–249.

Zebrowitz, Leslie A. *Reading Faces: Window to the Soul?*. New York: Westview Press, 1997.

BUY A SHARE OF THE FUTURE IN YOUR COMMUNITY

These certificates make great holiday, graduation and birthday gifts that can be personalized with the recipient's name. The cost of one S.H.A.R.E. or one square foot is $54.17. The personalized certificate is suitable for framing and will state the number of shares purchased and the amount of each share, as well as the recipient's name. The home that you participate in "building" will last for many years and will continue to grow in value.

Here is a sample SHARE certificate:

YES, I WOULD LIKE TO HELP!

I support the work that Habitat for Humanity does and I want to be part of the excitement! As a donor, I will receive periodic updates on your construction activities but, more importantly, I know my gift will help a family in our community realize the dream of homeownership. **I would like to SHARE in your efforts against substandard housing in my community!** *(Please print below)*

PLEASE SEND ME _____ SHARES at $54.17 EACH = $ $_____

In Honor Of: _____

Occasion: (Circle One)   HOLIDAY   BIRTHDAY   ANNIVERSARY

　　　　OTHER: _____

Address of Recipient: _____

Gift From: _____   *Donor Address:* _____

Donor Email: _____

I AM ENCLOSING A CHECK FOR $ $_____ PAYABLE TO HABITAT FOR HUMANITY OR PLEASE CHARGE MY VISA OR MASTERCARD *(CIRCLE ONE)*

Card Number _____   Expiration Date: _____

Name as it appears on Credit Card _____   Charge Amount $ _____

Signature _____

Billing Address _____

Telephone # Day _____   Eve _____

PLEASE NOTE: Your contribution is tax-deductible to the fullest extent allowed by law.
Habitat for Humanity • P.O. Box 1443 • Newport News, VA 23601 • 757-596-5553
www.HelpHabitatforHumanity.org

Printed in the United States
146491LV00001B/13/P